MERCIFUL
A Devotional Journal

MERCIFUL
A Devotional Journal

Susan G. Kabelitz

Merciful: A Devotional Journal
Copyright © 2023 by *Susan G. Kabelitz*

Published in the United States of America
ISBN   Paperback: 979-8-89091-029-5
ISBN   Hardback: 979-8-89091-030-1
ISBN   eBook: 979-8-89091-031-8

Scripture quotations are taken from the Holy Bible, Amplified Bible, copyright © 2015 by The Lockman Foundation. All rights reserved.

All rights reserved. No part of this publication may be reproduced, stored in a retrieval system or transmitted in any way by any means, electronic, mechanical, photocopy, recording or otherwise without the prior permission of the author except as provided by USA copyright law.

The opinions expressed by the author are not necessarily those of ReadersMagnet, LLC.

ReadersMagnet, LLC
10620 Treena Street, Suite 230 | San Diego, California, 92131 USA
1.619. 354. 2643 | www.readersmagnet.com

Book design copyright © 2023 by ReadersMagnet, LLC. All rights reserved.

Cover design by Ericka Obando
Interior design by Don De Guzman

MERCY
EXPRESSES
REVEALS
CHRIST'S
IMPERISHABLE
FRUITFUL
UNENDING
LOVE

By Susan G. Kabelitz

DAY 1

He is King Jesus. He is crowning us with His loving-kindness and tender mercy. Where do you wear a crown? It is wore upon your head. This implies His thoughts towards us are love and forgiveness.

According to the dictionary mercy is compassion or forgiveness shown towards someone whom it is within your power to punish or harm. Upon the time of salvation His mercy is slow to become angry. He does not keep account of our record of wrongs. He does not remember our sins because He lovingly forgives us and as *"far as the east is from the west so far has He removed our transgressions from us."* Psalm 103:10–12 (Amplified)

He is a loving Heavenly Father who has compassion for us. He delights in fellowshipping with us as His children.

➢ How does this make you feel knowing that Jesus the King crowns you with His loving-kindness and mercy?
_____
_____
_____
_____
_____

➢ How has it changed your relationship with Him?
_____
_____
_____
_____
_____

➢ How has it changed your relationship towards others?
_____
_____
_____
_____
_____

DAY 2

There is another aspect of mercy that is defined by a love that responds to human need in an unexpected or unmerited way. This is demonstrated in the story of the Samaritan.

A man was traveling from Jerusalem headed to Jericho. Robbers came stripping him of his clothing, his things and beat him leaving him lying there. There was no one to assist him to a doctor to heal him from the wounds incurred by the robbers.

A priest noticed him lying there but went on his way. But a certain Samaritan came being moved with compassion and mercy he humbled himself taking the time to dress the stranger's wounds. He poured oil and wine. He placed him on his beast. He took him to an inn and served him by attending to his wounds. He also paid for the expense of the inn giving it to the innkeeper. Then the Samaritan gave extra telling the innkeeper he would return to see if the stranger needed anything else. Luke 10:30-35 (Amplified)

➢ Do you know anyone like the Good Samaritan? If so who?

_____
_____
_____
_____
_____

➢ How has God been pouring His mercy into your life to share with a stranger that He leads you to?

_____
_____
_____
_____
_____

➢ How is God shaping your character to be more like Jesus?

_____
_____
_____
_____

DAY 3

In Psalm 9:9-10 the Lord is a refuge or a place of safety. He is a high tower to the afflicted. Affliction can come in the form of persecution, mental distress or prolonged sickness.

When you choose to surrender to God and allow Him to show himself strong on your behalf you get to know His name. Then through your personal walk with Him becoming closer to Him. He gives His mercy to you. He strengthens, comforts and heals you. He embraces you. The Lord never forsakes you because you looked to Him. He indeed is a place of safety and His name is trustworthy.

➤ How has God been a refuge to you?

_____
_____
_____
_____
_____

➤ How has surrendering to God helped you receive His mercy in your distress?

_____
_____
_____
_____
_____

➤ How did the Lord heal you? In what way has God changed your mind about affliction and turned it to a testimony of victory?

_____
_____
_____
_____
_____

DAY 4

Waiting upon the Lord is the anticipation that He is leading and guiding you to be and do while you remain peaceful, worshipful, listening to His voice for direction in your life. It is expecting His mercy and loving-kindness.

My heart is content in the Lord. It is thankful. You remain restful in Him, talking to Him and take the time to get to know Him. He is your help and shield.

"May Your mercy and loving-kindness, O Lord be upon us in proportion to our waiting and hoping for you."

—Psalm 33:18, 20-22 (Amplified)

➤ How have you been waiting upon the Lord?

_____
_____
_____
_____
_____

➤ How have you got to know Him in the process of waiting?

_____
_____
_____
_____
_____

➤ How have you seen His mercy in the process of waiting?

_____
_____
_____
_____
_____

DAY 5

Jesus has been an example of love and mercy. On the cross he said, *"Father, forgive them for they do not know what they have done."* Luke 27:24. He took upon Himself my sins and your sins when you receive His redemption by asking Him to forgive you for your sins. He becomes real. His Word comes alive.

He allows you to have a rich relationship with Him. The relationship grows and you desire to be pleasing and honoring to Him. His mercy forgives and is an important character quality that He implements through the Spirit of God and by applying the Word to your situation.

It is given as an appeal to those who receive God's mercy to commit your body, mind and heart to live a holy life apart from the world's ways. Thus, receiving guidance on a daily basis how He would direct your steps to be honorable to Him. Thereby, being a blessing back to Him and others is your reasonable service. Romans 12:1 & 2 (Amplified)

➢ How has Jesus' forgiveness impacted your life?
_____
_____
_____
_____
_____

➢ How have you chosen to forgive those who have wronged you?
_____
_____
_____
_____
_____

➢ How have you chosen to live your life in light of His mercy?
_____
_____
_____
_____
_____

➢ How has He transformed your mind concerning mercy? How has He transformed your heart into being merciful like Him?
_____
_____
_____
_____

DAY 6

In this life there are requirements in order to graduate from High School. Also there are requirements to graduate from college.

In order to work at a job there are requirements as well. There are entrance tests to take and pass to be employed.

What about God? He desires that your heart be right with Him. Jesus died on the cross for sin. We all fall short of the glory of God. Romans 6:23. Therefore, when you receive Jesus as Savior and Lord; He reveals the things that are necessary in order for us to be changed. According to Micah 6:8 "He has showed you, O man what is good. And what does the Lord require of you, but to do justly, and to love kindness and mercy and to humble yourself and walk humbly with your God?"

It is good and a requirement to be humble towards others. In order to live your life before God, He desires you to do that which is right. In addition, He loves it when you are merciful or do not respond in anger but, rather in love forgiving the person who may have treated you unkindly.

He desires us to walk humbly before God. This is being respectful of God and obeying Him because you love Him.

Thereby, spending time in His Word getting to know Him and His rich love and mercy that He has for you on a daily basis.

➢ What requirements have you had to do in order to graduate from college? Or in order to be employed?

_____
_____
_____
_____
_____

➢ What has the Lord required from you towards others?

_____
_____
_____
_____
_____

➢ What in your life has God been revealing to you about your relationship with Him?

_____
_____
_____
_____
_____

DAY 7

In this world there are changes occurring daily. There are differences of opinion. There is weather phenomenon happening. There are people who are left to defend for themselves. There are those who are poor. Many feel overwhelmed and need solutions.

Even David faced storms and difficulties in his life. It is stated in Psalm 57:1-2 *"Be merciful and gracious to me, O God, be merciful and gracious to me, for my soul takes refuge and finds shelter and confidence in you; yes, in the shadow of your wings will I take refuge and be confident until calamities and destructive storms are passed. I will cry to God Most High, who performs on my behalf and rewards me who brings to pass His purposes for me and surely completes them."*

When you run to God and spend time worshiping and focusing on His solution and in who God is; God becomes big. You are being quieted and embraced by His grace, love and mercy in your situation. Thereby, receiving His confidence to obtain your victory.

➢ Where do you run to when you find yourself in a storm?

_____
_____
_____
_____
_____

➢ How has God become your confidence in your situation?

_____
_____
_____
_____
_____

➢ How has God drawn near you while worshiping Him in your storm?

_____
_____
_____
_____
_____

➤ How have you felt Him surround you in your personal situation?

_____
_____
_____
_____
_____

➤ How was He merciful to you in the storm?

_____
_____
_____
_____
_____

DAY 8

The Lord is worthy. He is the giver of life. He is my song. David states in Psalm 89:1 *"I will sing of the mercy and loving-kindness of the Lord forever; with my mouth will I make known Your faithfulness from generation to generation."*

To sing to the Lord is an expression of praise. To worship the Lord is to bless Him with your heart. He loves it when you spend time seeking Him. This is done by sitting and listening to Him and through spending time in His Word. Then you respond back to Him loving, being sincere and doing what He says. He also loves it when you sing to Him. This is your heart responding to His love and mercy. It is also your heart communing with His heart. It brings moments of unity by surrendering and worshiping Him in song. It changes you, frees you and strengthens you. Thereby, allowing you to be like Him to those around you. It reassures you and reminds you that He indeed is merciful, loving and faithful.

➤ In your quiet time with the Lord how has it strengthened you?
_____
_____
_____
_____
_____
_____

➤ How has singing to Him changed your attitude?
_____
_____
_____
_____
_____
_____

➤ How has worshiping Him freed you to be more like Him?
_____
_____
_____
_____
_____
_____

➤ How have you seen His mercy and faithfulness in your life this week?
_____
_____
_____
_____
_____
_____

DAY 9

In life there are losses, sadness, disappointments and you can be discouraged.

Yet, in II Corinthians 1:3-4 it states *"Blessed be the God and Father of our Lord Jesus Christ, the Father of sympathy and the God of every comfort. Who comforts us in every trouble, so that we may also be able to comfort those who are in any kind of trouble or distress, with the comfort with which we ourselves are comforted by God."*

According to the dictionary to comfort means to alleviate or lessen the sadness. It also is to encourage or soothe. It can bring calm and gladden one's soul.

In these passages it states that God is the source of all comfort. He walks, talks and listens. He soothes us wrapping His loving arms around us. He loves us and gives us hope and encourages us. He brings others around us who have received His comfort and in turn we are able to console those He brings into our life's with His encouragement and comfort.

➢ How have you been comforted by God as Father?

___

➢ How has God encouraged you in your walk with Him?

___

➢ How have you noticed divine connections by God in your walk with Him?

___

DAY 10

Jeremiah was known as the weeping prophet. He witnessed devastation to Jerusalem. There was much affliction and no peace. There was much grief and captivity. The people had turned their heart away from God. Jeremiah seeks God; yet God shuts out his prayer. He continues to feel bitterness. He says, "God has covered me with ashes." Lamentations 3:16 mentions He feels no peace. In his mind he forgot what good and happiness are. He says, "He is bowed down within himself."

Yet, "I recall and therefore have I hope and expectation: It is because of the Lord's mercy and loving-kindness that we are not consumed, because His compassion's fail not. They are new every morning; great and abundant is Your stability and faithfulness."

"The Lord is my portion or share, also it states my living being; therefore will I hope in Him and wait expectantly for Him. The Lord is good to those who wait hopefully and expectantly for Him, to those who seek Him."

—Lamentations 3:22-25

You may be in a difficult situation finding yourself weeping and feeling no comfort or peace Yet, God's Word states, His mercies are new every morning and great is His faithfulness. Press into God and ask God to reveal to you His mercy for the day and His faithfulness in your situation. Thereby, I will hope and wait expectantly for Him for He is good to me.

➤ In life there can be difficult situations who do you run to? And why?

_____
_____
_____
_____
_____

➤ How have you recalled to your mind God's faithfulness in your situation?

_____
_____
_____
_____
_____

➤ How has He been faithful to you in the situation you may be in or have been in the past?

_____
_____
_____
_____
_____

➤ How have you seen His mercy today?

_____
_____
_____
_____

➢ How has He been good to you in the situation?

_____
_____
_____
_____
_____

DAY 11

In this life there can be affliction. It can come from self-reliance, being misunderstood or even physical pain upon your body. Still it happens.

It is stated in Psalm 34:19 "Many are the afflictions of the righteous but the Lord delivers them out of them all." In Isaiah 63 the people are being afflicted. Jesus reminds us in verse 8b He was a Savior in all their distresses. In verse 9 it states, "In all their affliction he was afflicted and the Angel of His presence saved them; in His love and His pity. He redeemed them; and He lifted them up and carried them all the days of old."

When we draw close to Jesus he comes close to us in our distress or affliction. He carries us through and He lovingly redeems and mends what needs to be healed.

Therefore, in the light of all of this Isaiah 63:7 states, "I will recount the loving-kindnesses of the Lord and the praiseworthy deeds of the Lord, according to all that the Lord has bestowed on us and the great goodness to the house of Israel, which He has granted them according to His mercy and according to the multitude of His loving-kindness."

➢ In your time of distress or affliction how did you allow Him to carry you?

_____
_____
_____
_____
_____

➢ How have you remembered His praiseworthy deeds and loving-kindness towards you in your distress or affliction?

_____
_____
_____
_____
_____

➢ How has He redeemed you in your situation?

_____
_____
_____
_____
_____

DAY 12

A priest was chosen to act on behalf of people pertaining to the matters of God. Yet, Jesus became our High Priest. He understands and took upon Himself our sin and weaknesses. He was tempted like us; yet He did not sin. He was dependent upon His Father God and prayed to Him continually. He didn't do anything without seeking God. He came boldly to the throne of grace. He is now our High Priest granting mercy for our failures and helping us to receive His grace to obtain in times of need. His grace comes when we pray to Him about the situation we may be in or facing. His Word is true and does not fail. It is alive and full of power. It is sharper than a two edge sword. It divides going deep between your soul and spirit. It exposes and judges your thoughts and motives of your heart.

Yet, God grants us His mercy and grace. Talking to Him and seeking His forgiveness and allowing Him to be close to us bringing His grace and mercy to others.

—Hebrews 4:12, 14-16 Hebrews 5:1

➢ How has Jesus become your High Priest?
_____
_____
_____
_____

➢ How have you obtained mercy and grace to help you in your time of need?
_____
_____
_____
_____

➢ How has God's Word changed you in your situation currently?
_____
_____
_____
_____

DAY 13

Moses was called by God to deliver the Israelite's from Egyptian bondage. God did miracles. He parted the Red Sea. Moses fasted and prayed. God wrote the Ten Commandments through Moses. He spent time talking to God getting the directives on behalf of the people.

In Psalm 90 it states, "Lord, You have been our dwelling place and our refuge in all generations."

You are God. We were dust and will go back to dust. Therefore, "Teach us to number our days that we may get us a heart of wisdom. O satisfy us with Your mercy and loving-kindness in the morning that we may rejoice and be glad all our days."

"Make us glad in proportion to the days in which You have afflicted us and to the years in which we have suffered evil. Let Your work be revealed to Your servants and Your majesty to their children. And let the beauty and delightfulness and favor of the Lord our God be upon us confirm and establish the work of our hands."

—Psalm 90:12,14-17 Amplified

Wisdom comes by seeking God's directive's. In life and in the past generations there were circumstances that God allowed. Yet as you cling to God. He satisfies you with His mercy every morning. He allows us to rejoice. He is loving and kind. May His work in this season of our life be revealed to you and your children and their children. Allow your grace and beauty to shine in our lives.

➢ How have you spent your time seeking God's directives for your life? What did He say?
_____
_____
_____
_____
_____

➢ How have you sought God on behalf of your family?
_____
_____
_____
_____
_____

➢ How has God allowed you to rejoice in Him?
_____
_____
_____
_____
_____

➢ How have you seen God's mercy in your life even in the difficult times?
_____
_____
_____
_____
_____

DAY 14

The Lord had mercy on Mary the mother of Jesus. She was just a teenager when the Holy Spirit came upon her and allowed her to be the mother of Jesus.

Mary's heart put God in the right perspective. She says, "My soul magnifies and extols the Lord, and my spirit rejoices in God my Savior."

God Almighty has done great things. Many people will be given spiritual life because God in His mercy will redeem lives that call upon Him and accept His gift of salvation. He has mercy upon those who humble themselves and stay in awe of God. They willingly yield their lives to the service of Him. He communicates with them and they rejoice like Mary as God is honored.

Jesus came, "To bring and give the knowledge of salvation to His people in the forgiveness and remission of their sins. Because of and through the heart of tender mercy and loving-kindness of our God, a light from on high will dawn upon us and visit us." Luke 1:46,47,50,77 & 78 Amplified

➢ What happened to Mary the mother of Jesus?
_____
_____
_____
_____
_____

➢ How has God's salvation made a difference in your life?
_____
_____
_____
_____
_____

➢ What great things has He done for you?
_____
_____
_____
_____
_____

DAY 15

"The Lord is good to all and His tender mercies are over all His works." Psalm 145:9

When you think of work you think about a job. A job like cleaning your house or doing the gardening. This takes time, finances and effort to do the job well. These jobs are also on going. There is maintenance to keeping your house clean. The garden will grow weeds on their own. This is just like dust it is continuous.

According to God's Word his kind mercy is upon His creation.

It is exhibited looking at the ocean, rotation of the seasons bringing the springtime full of flowers and trees. The sun comes up daily keeping us warm. The ground yields its vegetation and fruit. This allows us to eat. The water and soil give moisture and nutrients to harvest the crop.

Yes, the Lord is good to us daily. Thereby, receiving His tender mercies' by living on the earth.

➤ How have you noticed His tender mercy in God's works?

_____
_____
_____
_____
_____

➤ How have you noticed God's mercy in the seasons?

_____
_____
_____
_____
_____

➤ How have you noticed God's mercy at your job or volunteer work?

_____
_____
_____
_____
_____

DAY 16

In life there are laws to abide by for personal safety. They are there as boundaries. The Ten Commandments were given showing man they needed rules and standards to live by. However, man fell short of these standards. According to Hebrews 7:19 it states, "For the Law never made anything perfect but instead a better hope is introduced through which we [now] come close to God."

"But God so rich is He in His mercy! Because of and in order to satisfy the great and wonderful and intense love with which He loved us. Even when we were dead by shortcomings and trespasses; He made us alive together in fellowship and in union with Christ. He gave us the very life of Christ Himself, the same new life with which He quickened Him, for it is by grace (His favor and mercy which you did not deserve) that you are saved (delivered from judgment and made partakers of Christ's salvation. For by grace have we been saved through faith and not by works or keeping standards. It is not of yourself it is a gift from God lest anyone boast." Ephesians 2:4, 5, 8, and 9.

Wow God is amazing. He in love and mercy thought of us when we broke all the standards and could not measure up. He delivered us from the penalty of sin or judgment for our sins. When we received His gift we are unable to boast that we saved ourselves. Instead, Christ became the perfect sacrifice for sin. He knew no sin. He resurrected and He made us alive to spend eternity with Him.

➢ How has God taught you about standards in this life?

___

➢ How did God reveal himself to you that you fell short of His standards?

___

➢ What happened to you as a result of receiving a personal relationship with God? How did you change?

___

➢ How did you handle His love and mercy? Do you appreciate it and demonstrate it to those in your sphere of influence? If so share how?

___

DAY 17

God's mercy keeps on going. It is felt, experienced and received.

Joseph served Potiphar the officer of Pharaoh in Egypt. He became a supervisor. He ate well. He was very good looking in appearance. He fled from Potiphar and was not willing to break apart a marriage by giving into temptation. Yet, Potiphar believed the lies of his wife therefore, Joseph found himself in prison.

In Genesis 39:21 it states that the Lord was with Joseph and showed him mercy and loving-kindness and gave him favor in the sight of the warden of the prison.

There can be situations in your life that you may be doing the correct thing yet, to others it is not believed. It is in those times you have the opportunity to not react or speak ill of. It is in those times that God's mercy and loving-kindness can launch you to your God given destiny. Thereby, receiving favor by not reacting but, instead continuing to do right by honoring God.

➢ How have you experienced God's mercy in your prison?

_____

➢ Have you been in a situation that you chose to honor God but people misunderstood you and so you chose to forgive and keep a Godly attitude? If so explain?

_____

➢ How did God turn your prison into a palace or it became your destiny?

_____

DAY 18

David is praying. He is poor. He is having trouble. He is dedicated. He is God's servant. He is looking to God and trusts Him.

In Psalm 86: 3 & 4 it states, "Be merciful and gracious to me, O Lord, for to You do I cry all day. Make me Your servant to rejoice, O Lord, for to You do I lift myself up."

He says that God is good and does forgive. God is full of mercy and loving-kindness to everyone who calls upon Him.

David in verse 12 praises God with His whole heart and will bring glory to God's name forever.

He understands and accepts God's great mercy and loving-kindness towards him. God has delivered him from the depths of affliction.

He also knows where He receives strength from and knows that it is God who helps Him and comforts him in his time of trouble.

Therefore, God will be merciful and cause me to rejoice and I will praise and glorify His name forever.

➢ In your trouble how are you receiving His mercy and loving-kindness?
___
___
___
___
___

➢ Is God your strength? If so how?
___
___
___
___
___

➢ How has God caused you to rejoice giving Him glory in delivering you from the depths of affliction?
___
___
___
___
___

DAY 19

According to Psalm 52 it is not in the best interest of a person to love evil more than good. It is not good to lie and speak hurtful. It will bring scoffing. It is not wise to not allow God to be your strength. It is not wise to place your trust in the abundance of riches causing you to feel secure in your wealth through wickedness.

According to verse 8 & 9 But instead, "I am like a green olive tree in the house of God. I trust in and confidently rely on the loving-kindness and mercy of God forever and ever. I will thank You and confide in You forever, because You have done it [delivered me and kept me safe]. I will wait on, hope in and expect in Your name, for it is good, in the presence of Your saints (Your kind and pious ones)."

Therefore, I will allow God to be my strength, confidence and will always confide in Him in every manner concerning issues of life. He will be loving and show me His mercy forever and ever.

➢ How have you allowed God to be your strength in your life this week?

_____
_____
_____
_____
_____

➢ How have you allowed God to love you and have mercy in your financial situation?

_____
_____
_____
_____
_____

➢ How has He been faithful to you this week?

_____
_____
_____
_____
_____

DAY 20

Paul was an apostle called by God.

Mercy can be displayed in your prayers on behalf of others. Some people come into your life to serve and help the leader like Paul.

According to II Timothy 1:16-18 it states, "May the Lord grant [His] mercy to the family of Onesiphorus, for he often showed me kindness and ministered to my needs [comforting and reviving and bracing me like fresh air]! He was not ashamed of my chains and imprisonment [for Christ's sake.] No, rather when he reached Rome, he searched diligently and eagerly for me and found me. May the Lord grant to him that he may find mercy from the Lord on that [great] day! And you know how many things he did for me and what a help he was at Ephesus [you know better than I can tell you]."

Some people are called to be compassionate and helpful rather than being the leader. Yet, to God and the leader they may be supporting they are both equally important.

Paul appreciated Onesiphorus and his family. He asked God to be merciful to Onesiphorus when He sees God in heaven. "Blessed are the merciful for they shall obtain mercy." Matthew 5:7

May you pray for your family and friends who are merciful and kind. May God reveal Himself to them and be merciful to them.

➢ Who in your life has been merciful to you?
_____
_____
_____
_____

➢ How did they show it to you?
_____
_____
_____
_____

➢ How do Paul and Onesiphorus compliment each other?
_____
_____
_____
_____

DAY 21

Rejoicing comes when you have gone through a trial and count it all joy. Rejoicing comes when you marry the love of your life and get to celebrate old age together.

Rejoicing comes when you work at a job that is successful and you put your service and efforts in for thirty plus years and retire.

For David in Psalm 21 He rejoiced in God's power or strength. God gave him many victories. He prayed to God and God gave him his heart's desire. God blessed him richly and gave him long life. He delighted greatly in being in God's presence. He learned to trust God and receive God's unfailing love. He committed everything to God laying it at His feet allowing God to give him wisdom to receive victory.

Because of God's steadfast love and mercy that never fails David became unmovable. God handled his enemies.

Therefore, like David you can rejoice, be blessed and experience God's steadfast love and mercy in your life bringing rejoicing to your life and other's life's as well.

➢ How has God brought rejoicing to you?

___

➢ How can you relate to David when you trusted in God's unfailing love in your situation?

___

➢ How has God been merciful to you when you talked to Him and sought His wisdom in your situation?

___

DAY 22

To be thankful is to appreciate and be content with the many ways the Lord and others bless you.

It is also remembering the good and knowing that God is working for your good. There can be trying times. Even still, past generations endured many difficult times and yet, the redeemed one's cried to the Lord and He delivered them from the hand of the enemy.

In Psalm 107 they cried to the Lord and He delivered them out of their distress. He led them forth by the straight and right way, that they might go to a city where they could establish their homes.

Let's praise the Lord for His goodness and loving-kindness and His wonderful works to the children of men. "For He satisfies the longing soul and fills the hungry soul with good."

Yes, God is merciful and causes you to be content, thankful and reminds you that He is the deliverer and lifts up the hungry soul bringing good to your situation in your life and in the lives of those in your sphere of influence.

➢ How did God remind you to be thankful?

_____
_____
_____
_____
_____

➢ How did the Lord show His mercy and loving-kindness by delivering you in your situation?

_____
_____
_____
_____
_____

➢ How did He show you the right way? How did God satisfy your hungry soul with good?

_____
_____
_____
_____
_____

DAY 23

David was a shepherd boy who took care of sheep.

Psalm 23 is a word picture that is describing God our Lord who is our Shepherd. He meets our needs by clothing and feeding us.

He allows to be among green pastures; He directs your steps beside peaceful and restful waters.

God revives and heals you. God directs you to His path of righteousness because He is the Good Shepherd.

There can be times of experiencing the shadow of death Yet, God tells you to not fear because He is with you. His rod protects and guides thereby, experiencing comfort.

God prepares a table or a feast of His presence. This causes you to remember He is good and will take care of your enemies. The Holy Spirit gives you God's thoughts.

Yes, goodness, mercy and His unfailing love go behind you and surround you all your days on this earth.

Looking forward to being in the house of the Lord where His presence dwells continually forever and ever. Amen.

➤ How have you experienced God meeting your needs?

___

➤ How did God lead you beside still and restful waters?

___

➤ When you sought the Lord for His healing how did it manifest?

___

➤ How did God prepare a table before you in the midst of your enemies?

___

➢ How have you experienced God's goodness and mercy in your journey with Him?

_____
_____
_____
_____
_____

➢ Have you enjoyed God's presence by meeting with Him? If so explain.

_____
_____
_____
_____
_____

DAY 24

In your life clothes are important to wear. They can be an expression of who you are as a person.

God's word in Colossians 3:12 states, "As God's chosen people, holy and dearly loved clothe yourselves with compassion, kindness, humility, gentleness and patience."

It is important to put on compassion and not be unkind. God is love and compassionate and you represent Him to the world.

In addition, Proverbs 3:3 states, "Let love and faithfulness never leave you; bind them around your neck, write them on the tablet of your heart."

The neck is what turns your head and your mind is what you use to make decisions. Therefore, allow your mind to be kind and allow your heart to be compassionate and loving to yourself and others.

According to Proverbs 3:4 "Then you will win favor and a good name in the sight of God and man."

➢ Clothes matter to God and mankind what kind are you wearing physically?

_____
_____
_____
_____
_____

➢ Clothes matter to God and mankind what kind are you wearing spiritually in your attitude towards yourself and others?

_____
_____
_____
_____
_____

➢ Between you and God if your attitude has not been loving, kind and compassionate towards others take this time to ask for God's forgiveness and ask Him to help you be loving, kind and forgiving.

_____
_____
_____
_____

DAY 25

Loving God and mankind will be rewarded. Every kind word, act of service to others as well as honoring your parents will be rewarded.

According to Psalm 62:12 which states, "O Lord belong mercy and loving-kindness for You render to every man according to his work."

In Revelation 22:12 it states, "Behold, I am coming soon, and I shall bring My rewards with Me, to repay and render to each one just what his own actions and his own work merit."

In II Thessalonians 3:12b & 13 He exhorts you as a minister in doing God's work to do it in quietness and earn your own food and other necessities. He also exhorts you to not get weary or lose heart in doing right.

Everything that you do to honor God and to love people in private will be noticed by God. He is coming real soon. He is your source and because of Him you move and have your being in Him.

Therefore, occupy until He comes and continue to bless God by being a blessing to others in His love.

➢ What work do you do for Jesus?

___

➢ How has God allowed you to quietly render service to others?

___

➢ How has God or others encouraged you in your work or ministry for Him?

___

➢ Jesus says, He is coming soon with His rewards. How has this motivated you to keep working for His glory?

___

DAY 26

In Matthew 18:21-35 Peter asked Jesus how many times do you need to forgive or release anything you may have against someone? His answer is seventy times seven. This means infinity or continuous when necessary. This passage continues to use an analogy to describe the kingdom of heaven. It is like a human king who one is choosing to forgive a debt by receiving a settlement. And the other is demanding payment that he or she can not repay. This person was thrown in jail to be tortured until He pays back the debt by spending time concerning a judgment that was rendered.

These are examples of mercy or torture. God in the next passage states, "This is how my heavenly Father will treat each of you unless you forgive your brother or sister from your heart."

Forgiveness is a chose you make to forgive and extend mercy or pardon to the person that you wronged or they wronged you.

Whenever you allow your flesh to have its way and become angry or bitter it leads to judgment or torture.

Therefore, choose to forgive and receive mercy rather than judgment or being in a prison of torture.

Thereby, in Romans 13:8, "Owe no man any debt but rather love each other from the heart."

➢ How many times must a person forgive?

_____
_____
_____
_____
_____

➢ Explain how important it is to extend mercy by forgiving? What happens when you choose not to forgive?

_____
_____
_____
_____
_____

➢ What is God asking and desiring for you to do according to Romans 13:8?

_____
_____
_____
_____
_____

DAY 27

In the book of Numbers 6:24-27 it states, *"The Lord bless you and watch, guard, and keep you; The Lord makes His face to shine upon and enlighten you and be gracious to you;*

The Lord lift up His [approving countenance upon you and give you peace (tranquility of heart and life continually).

And they shall put My name upon the Israelites, and I will bless them."

This prayer is prayed and is called the Aaronite blessing for the people of God and the Israelites.

They receive blessing by God looking out for them and He protects and gives them life. May His face of His glory or goodness along with His wisdom and discernment be yours from Him. May you have His Shalom or peace. His peace extends to your mind, heart, body and circumstances. His peace guides you to make Godly right decisions. May His presence rest upon you as you seek Him. He gives you favor, is merciful, kind and loving.

God's name is upon the Israelites and He does bless His people.

David in Psalm 67:1 prays that God would bless you. He is blessing you by being gracious to you. He is causing His face or His presence to be in you and among you. May you be confident that He is showing His favor upon you and extending His peace all the days of your life.

➢ According to Numbers 6:24 what is God doing for you?

___

➢ According to Numbers 6:25 what is God doing to your soul? Your mind and body? What is He doing in your circumstances?

___

➢ How has God been gracious to you by being in His presence?

___

➢ Can you relate to David's prayer in Psalm 67:1? If so how?

___

DAY 28

There can be times in your life that you are doing what God's plans and purposes are in your life. Yet, like Job the Lord said to Satan; "Have you considered my servant Job, that there is none like him on the earth, a blameless and upright man, one who fears God and abstains from and shuns evil." Job 1:8

God had placed a hedge of protection around him, his house and all that He owned. God increased him.

In the story of Job, God tested him. God knew that he is a righteous man who loves and honors God. His friends, wife and others were no comfort. Yet, according to Job 19:25, 26b Job says, "I know my Redeemer and Vindicator lives. In addition, after Job dies He shall see God."

Job suffered in his body and loss his children. He lost his fortunes.

God revealed to Job in Job Job 42:5-6; "I had heard of you [only] by the hearing of the ear, but now my spiritual eyes see You. Therefore, I loathe [my words] and abhor myself and repent in dust and ashes."

Sometimes God allows you to see yourself and the words you may have spoken. Even though things are going well on the outside your inside may need God to reveal to you your need for Him to heal, restore and you may need to repent from anything that you may have said. Also, you may need to pray for your friends.

In Job 42:10-12 it states, "And the Lord turned the captivity of Job and restored his fortunes, when he prayed for his friends; Also the Lord gave Job twice as much as he had before. Then there came to him all his brothers and sisters and all who had known him before and they ate bread with him and comforted him over all the [distressing] calamities that the Lord had brought upon him. Every man also gave him a piece of money, and every man an earring of gold. And the Lord blessed the latter days of Job more than his beginning."

According to James 5:11 Job endured. God's purpose was fulfilled. He was blessed in the end of his life, "in as much as the Lord is full of pity and compassion and tenderness and mercy."

It is important to remember that no matter what you may be going through God has plenty of compassion, love and mercy and He lives and is your Redeemer.

➢ Job was tested by God what happened during the testing?

➢ How did Job respond according to Job 42:5 & 6?

➢ Between you and God, is there anything He is revealing to you that needs Him to heal or you need to repent for? If so explain.

➢ How was Job's life, fortunes and captivity changed according to Job 42:10-12?

➢ How has God been merciful to you in your captivity?

_____
_____
_____
_____
_____
_____

➢ How did God bring restoration and become your Redeemer?

_____
_____
_____
_____
_____
_____

DAY 29

In life's situations people seek to earn your trust. Whenever you decide to take out a loan for credit they are trusting that you will pay them back.

At the time of birth as an infant you trust your parents to feed, change your diapers, keep you clothed and meet your needs.

Trust means you rest in and know your loving Heavenly Father will clothe and take care of you.

In Proverbs 3:5 it states, "Lean on trust in, and be confident in the Lord with all your heart and mind and do not rely on your own insight or understanding."

To be confident in the Lord means you are joyful, peaceful and sure that God is good and faithful. His ways are best.

It is human nature that wants to figure out how God is working or moving in your situation. It is also human nature that worry's or wants to control your situation rather than trust and receive that God is meeting your needs and He is faithful.

In Psalm 32:10b it says, "But he who trusts in relies on, and confidently leans on the Lord shall be compassed about with mercy and with loving-kindness."

Therefore, trust in the Lord and he will surround you with His mercy and loving-kindness. He is a loving Heavenly Father who protects you and brings good to your life.

➢ What is the world's way of trusting you?

___

➢ What is leaning on your own understanding?

___

➢ Explain a situation that you trusted God what was the outcome?

DAY 30

According to Psalm 119:105 it states, "Your word is a lamp to my feet and a light to my path."

God's word is magnified above His name. God's word is truth, life and all His promises are yes and amen. II Corinthians 1:20

Whenever you apply a promise from God's Word it can revive. It can heal, encourage, give wisdom and empower you with his strength. It can teach you right from wrong. It can enlighten you how much God loves you and He is faithful.

In light of all this, "I will praise you O Lord with all my heart. I will sing to you Lord. Like David, I will joyfully celebrate His mighty acts, for great is the glory of the Lord.

I will praise you for your loving-kindness and for your truth and faithfulness." Psalm 138:1-5

According to Psalm 138:8; The Lord will perfect that which concerns me; Your mercy and loving-kindness, O Lord, endure forever.

God's Word is high and full of integrity. God's mercy and loving-kindness goes on and on forever and ever. Amen.

➢ What is God's Word according to Psalm 119:105?

_____
_____
_____
_____
_____

➢ What can God's Word do when you stand on the promises?

_____
_____
_____
_____
_____

➢ And what did it do for you in the situation? Explain the difference between God's Word being magnified and His mercy and loving-kindness toward you?

_____
_____
_____
_____
_____

DAY 31

There are character qualities that at the time of salvation the Holy Spirit pours into our hearts.

According to Romans 5:5b "For God's love has been poured out in our hearts through the Holy Spirit who has been given to us."

God's love was exhibited through His Son Jesus the Christ. According to Romans 5:8 it states, "But God shows and clearly proves His love for us by the fact that while we were still sinners, Christ (the Messiah. The Anointed One) died for us." He gave His very best by surrendering to the will of God by shedding His blood. He sacrificed His life so that we can experience redemptive love and not receive God's wrath.

Jesus reconciled us back to the Father when we accept His gift of salvation. This gives us a relationship in which He first loved us, according to I John 4:10, "In this is love: not that we loved God, but that He loved us and sent His Son to be the propitiation (the atoning sacrifice) for our sins."

His love He gave and it is to be received. When you receive His love it aids you to love others and yourself. His love was sacrificial, demonstrated on the cross and forgave you for your sins. His love is endless.

➢ How does Jesus' love cause you to enter into a richer relationship with Him?
___
___
___
___
___

➢ How did Jesus reveal His love to you this week?
___
___
___
___
___

➢ How does knowing that Jesus loves you make you want to allow His Holy Spirit to pour even more love into you so that you can demonstrate His love to those around you?
___
___
___
___
___

DAY 32

In this life people like doctors, nurses and policemen serve people demonstrating love in a practical way. Firemen and the paramedics also risk their lives for the life of another. This is demonstrating love for another person.

According to Romans 12:7 it states [He whose gift is] practical service, let him give himself to serving.

Other ways of serving are volunteering for a food bank by giving out food to those in need.

Still another way of demonstrating love is working at a restaurant serving food to the people at the table who they are serving. They take the people's order and then the cook cooks the food. Then the waitress or waiter serves the food to the people at the table. The waitress or waiter listens to details of how the person wants their order. Thereby, showing love to the customer.

The Mercy Navel Ship is here to aid the Los Angeles community. The navy is serving in aiding people in getting well and is demonstrating love through a naval ship that is a hospital on a ship from San Diego, CA.

It is with much gratitude to all these services that aid the community in love through their services to people.

➢ Do you have a testimony of a service that helped you in your time of need? If so explain.
___
___
___
___
___

➢ How has God allowed you to do service in a restaurant or fast food service?
___
___
___
___
___

➢ Love is expressed through service of aiding the poor how has God allowed you to be a part of volunteering to feed people at a food bank or at a church?
___
___
___
___
___

DAY 33

In these times of uncertainty there is God and His love that can not separate us from Him and His love for us.

According to Romans 8:35 it states, "Who shall ever separate us from Christ's love? Shall suffering and affliction and tribulation? Or calamity and distress? Or persecution or hunger or destitution or peril or sword?"

None of these things can separate us from His love. His love is unconditional. It is not based on what you do or accomplish. It is not based if you attend church or you are not a person who attends church. He freely bestows His love to us.

During times of testing like medical emergencies and people experiencing tragedy. His love remains. He is close to those who draw near to Him. His love comforts, provides, strengthens and understands. He weeps with those who weep. He brings peace and joy in the midst of the trial.

According to Romans 8:37-39 it states, "Yet amid all these things we are more than conquerors and gain a surpassing victory through Him who loved us. For I am persuaded beyond doubt (am sure) that neither death nor life, nor angels, nor principalities, nor things impending and threatening nor things to come, nor powers, nor height, nor depth, nor anything else in all creation will be able to separate us from the love of God which is in Christ Jesus our Lord."

Therefore, in times of uncertainty His promise remains nothing can separate us from His love.

➢ When going through situations how has God been there for you?
___

➢ How did He show you His love?
___

➢ What is promised according to Romans 8:37?
___

➢ How has God persuaded you beyond doubt that He loves you?
___

DAY 34

In the natural a heart would be a picture of love. God has a bigger picture of what love is and how it is shown to mankind.

According to I Corinthians 13:4-8, "Love is patient, love is kind. It does not envy, it does not boast, it is not proud. It is not rude, it is not self-seeking, it is not easily angered, it keeps no record of wrongs. Love does not delight in evil but rejoices with the truth. It always protects, always trusts, always hopes, always perseveres. Love never fails."

A person who displayed these qualities in their life was Jesus while He lived on the earth and did ministry. He was patient on the cross, no unkind word came from His mouth. He was not jealous. He was humble and became obedient even to the death of the cross. He was not self-seeking, but rather He did miracles through listening and obeying His Father displaying trust and confidence in His Father and His will. He freely forgave those who wronged Him. He rejoiced in the truth and because of his actions of love He never failed.

In our lives we need the Spirit of God and daily need to yield to Him and thereby, His love will be in our life to love others as Jesus loved.

➢ What is a natural picture of love?

_____
_____
_____
_____
_____

➢ What is Jesus' picture of love or character qualities of love according to I Corinthians 13:4-8?

_____
_____
_____
_____
_____

➢ In what way is God's Spirit operating love through you this week?

_____
_____
_____
_____

DAY 35

There are some people who are ungrateful, selfish and wicked. These people would be considered your enemy. God tells us to love your enemies. It is shown by kind words and actions. Also, by not reacting to their selfish and harsh unkind words and actions. It is important to be the light and give to those who are in need without expecting interest or brownie points for your actions. God will bless you in secret.

Luke 6:27-32 states, "But I tell you who hear me; love your enemies, do good to those who hate you, bless those who curse you, pray for those who mistreat you. If someone strikes you on one cheek, turn to him the other also. If someone takes your cloak, do not stop him from taking your tunic. Give to everyone who asks you, and if anyone takes what belongs to you, do not demand it back. Do to others as you would have them do to you."

Love can be challenging but it is a kind word that turns away anger. Proverbs 15:1a

Luke 6:32-36 continues by saying, "If you love those who love you, what credit is that to you? Even sinners love those who love them. And if you do good to those who are good to you, what credit is that to you? Even 'sinners' lend to 'sinners,' expecting to be repaid in full. But love your enemies, do good to them and lend to them without expecting to get anything back. Then your reward will be great, and you will be sons of then Most High, because he is kind to the ungrateful and wicked. Be merciful, just as your Father is merciful."

Christ's love is unconditional. It is not based on how others act or treat you. Love gives to your enemies when wrongfully misused. Love is not revengeful. Love will always stand in any situation. Loving your enemy is done with Christ's love. The Spirit of God ruling in your heart and not your flesh. It is done in faith remembering Jesus sacrificed His life on the cross. He was demonstrating love to all the world. Thereby, allowing us to be forgiven and receive everlasting life. This indeed is true love.

➤ Who is your enemy?

___

➤ How are you to treat your enemy according to Luke 6:27- 36?

___

➤ According to Proverbs 15:1a what turns anger away?

___

➤ How did Christ treat His enemy on the cross? And what was the result?

___

DAY 36

Jesus answered a Pharisee who He knew was testing Him concerning the law. He asked Jesus; What is the greatest commandment in the law?

It is written in Matthew 22:37- 40, *"Love the Lord your God with all your heart and with all your soul and with all your mind. This is the first and greatest commandment.*

And the second is like it: Love your neighbor as yourself. All the Law and the Prophets hang on these two commandments."

To love God with all your heart means to obey Him. According to John 14:21 "whoever has my commands and obeys them, he is the one who loves me."

To love God with all your soul means to surrender your desires and plans to Him. He opens the doors and leads you into His destiny for your life. According to Galatians 2:20; "I have been crucified with Christ and I no longer live, but Christ lives in me. The life I live in the body, I live by faith in the Son of God who loved me and gave Himself for me."

To love God with all your mind means to give Him your thoughts and yield to His thoughts. His thoughts are love, joy, peace, patience, kindness, goodness, faithfulness, gentleness and self-control. Galatians 5:22 is also the fruits of the Spirit.

To love yourself as you love your neighbor means to nurture yourself in God's love. It is to not neglect taking care of yourself. It is to know that your body is the temple of God. His presence lives in you. Therefore, glorify God in your body.

To love your neighbor means to serve them in love. Be sensitive to their needs and call them on the phone or be an encouragement to them. Be a listening ear to someone who may be sick and pray for them to be healed. Rejoice with your neighbor during good times as well.

Therefore, let's love like Jesus demonstrating the greatest commandment: Love for Him, others and yourself for His glory.

➤ What question did the Pharisee ask?

___

➤ What did Jesus reply to the Pharisee?

___

➤ How do you love God?

___

➤ How do you love others?

___

➤ How do you love yourself?

___

DAY 37

Jehoshaphat reigned in Asa's stead. The Lord was with Jehoshaphat. He had great riches and honor. He honored God with all his heart, mind and soul. He set up a fast to seek the Lord concerning Judah. The Moabites, Ammonites and the Meunites came against Jehoshaphat to battle.

Jehoshaphat stood firm in the assembly of Judah and Jerusalem in the house of the Lord before the court. According to II Chronicles 20:6; He said, "O Lord, God of our fathers, are You not God in heaven? And do You not rule over all the Kingdoms of the nations? In Your hand are power and might, so that none is able to withstand You."

He continues by remembering God's faithfulness to them in the past. He states, "This land was given forever to the descendants of Abraham God's friend." They lived in the land and built you a place of worship for Your name. According to II Chronicles 20:9, "If evil comes upon us, the sword of judgment, or pestilence or famine, we will stand before this house and before You for Your Name is in this house and cry to You in our affliction, and You will hear and save." II Chronicles 20:12 continues by saying, "O our God, will You not exercise judgment upon them? For we have no might to stand against this great company that is coming against us. We do not know what to do but our eyes are upon You.."

II Chronicles 20:15 states, Hear all Judah you inhabitants of Jerusalem, and you King Jehoshaphat.. The Lord says, this to you: Be not afraid or dismayed at this great multitude; for the battle is not yours, but God's. And then verse 17 says, "You shall not need to fight in this battle: take your positions, stand still, and see the deliverance of the Lord [who is] with you, O Judah and Jerusalem. Fear not nor be dismayed. Tomorrow go out against them, for the Lord is with you." What was Jehoshaphat's response and action? He bowed his head with his face to the ground. Also all of Judah and the inhabitants of Jerusalem fell down before the Lord worshiping Him. Others did likewise the Levites of Kohathites and Korahites stood up to praise the Lord in a very loud voice.

Then verse 21 says, "When he had consulted with the people, He appointed singers to sing to the Lord and praise Him in their Holy garments as they went out before the army, saying, "Give thanks to the Lord, for His mercy and loving-kindness endure forever! And when they began to sing and to praise the Lord set ambushments against the men of Ammon, Moab and Mount Seir who come against Judah and they were [self-] slaughtered.

Hence, Jehoshaphat and his people took the spoil. It was more than they could carry away. It was three days in collecting the goods and spoil. They were so blessed that the place is called, Valley of Beracah or blessing. They returned with great rejoicing to the Lord for He had made them rejoice over their enemies. They played instruments such as harps, lyres and trumpets praising the Lord! God brought peace and rest around them.

There can be a battle raging around you. He reminds us to not fear. He also tells us in II Timothy 1:7, "God has not given us a Spirit of fear but of love, power and a sound mind."

It is important to keep our eyes on the Lord. Seek Him, worship Him with instruments and in song. Remember the battle is not ours but is the Lord's. Therefore, allow His thoughts of peace and love. Thereby, receiving the victory in Jesus' mighty and merciful name. Amen.

➤ According to II Chronicles 17:3,4 why was God with Jehoshaphat?

___

➤ Why did Jehoshaphat proclaim a fast in all Judah?

___

➤ According to II Chronicles 20:12 what happened?

___

➤ According to II Chronicles 20:15 what did the Lord say? What happened when Jehoshaphat and Judah, Levites of Kohathites as well as others praised and worshiped God?

___

➢ What was the result in verse 21?

➢ How did God speak to you during spending time with Him doing this lesson?

DAY 38

According to Proverbs 12:1 it states, *"Whoever loves discipline loves knowledge, but he who hates correction is stupid."*

To love discipline is to receive correction and instruction in the affairs of life.

According to Hebrews 12:5 & 6 it states, "My son or daughter, do not make light of the Lord's discipline and do not lose heart when he rebukes you, because the Lord disciplines those He loves, and he punishes everyone He accepts as a son.

God loves His children. It matters to Him because He is holy and as His children it is important to honor and obey leaders, supervisors, managers and your parents. Discipline is there to instruct or correct you to be all that God desires for you to be.

According to Hebrews 12:7-11 it states, "Endure hardship as discipline; God is treating you as sons for what son is not disciplined by his father? If you are not disciplined (and everyone undergoes discipline) then you are legitimate children and not true sons. Moreover, we have all had human fathers who disciplined us and we respected them for it. How much more should we submit to the Father of our spirit and live! Our fathers disciplined us for a little while as they thought best; but God disciplines us for our good, that we may share in His holiness. No discipline seems pleasant at the time, but painful. Later on, however, it produces a harvest of righteousness and peace for those who have been trained by it."

God treats you as sons. He disciplines you for your good. While being disciplined it can be hard but saying no to the flesh and allowing it to die brings life from God. The fruit of discipline is peace for those who allow and are taught by God. It yields to His fruit of right acting or being holy even as God would have you holy.

➤ What does Proverbs 12:1 say?

___

➤ When you are disciplined by God as a son according to Hebrews 12:5 & 6 what happens?

___

➤ What is the result of discipline according to Hebrews 5:11?

___

➤ Why be holy?

___

DAY 39

Faith comes by hearing and hearing by the word of God. Romans 10:17. As a believer we live by faith through love. Galatians 5:6. Spending time with the Lord in His word and obeying the promise is faith. Isaiah 55:11 states, "So shall My word be that goes forth out of My mouth: it shall not return to Me void [without producing any effect, useless], but it shall not return to Me void [without producing any effect, useless] but it shall accomplish that which I please and purpose, and it shall prosper in the thing for which I sent it."

God loves us so much that He has given us His word so that by exercising that word He gives you His power and strength through His Spirit to carry out that word for your situation. It is then you rest in his love and trust Him to carry it out.

According to I John 4:18 it states, "There is no fear in love, but full grown (complete, perfect) love turns fear out doors and expels every trace of terror! For fear brings with it the thought of punishment and [so] he who is afraid has not reached the full maturity of love.

According to I John 5:2-4 it states, "By this we came to know that we love the children of God: when we love God and obey His command's… For love of God is this: that we do His commands [keep] His ordinances and are mindful of His precepts and teaching]… For whatever is born of God is victorious over the world; and this is the victory that conquers the world even our faith."

Therefore, as His children we ask Him daily for more of His love and we live by faith and not by sight. We will live and move and have our being in Him. We will stand on the promises of God's word thereby, receive His victory.

➢ How does faith come according to Romans 10:17?

_____
_____
_____
_____

➢ According to I John 5:2 & 3 how do you know that you love God and His people?

_____
_____
_____
_____

➢ What is the victory that overcomes the world according to I John 5:4?

_____
_____
_____
_____

➢ How does faith work through love?

_____
_____
_____
_____

➢ What did God's Spirit teach you by doing this lesson?

_____
_____
_____

DAY 40

I John 2:15-17 states "Do not love or cherish the world or the things that are in the world. If anyone loves the world, love for the Father is not in him. For all that is in the world-the lust of the flesh [craving for sensual gratification] and the lust of the eyes [greedy longings of the mind] and the pride of life [assurance in one's own resources or in the stability of earthly things]-these do not come from the Father but are from the world [itself] And the world passes away and disappears and with it the forbidden cravings (the passionate desires the lust of it, but he who does the will of God and carries out His purposes in his life abides (remains) forever.

As a believer it is not God's will that you love the world. To love the ways of the world is to lust after the things in the world. It is to not walk in self-control and not care for those in need. You want things more than you want God and a relationship with Him. Also, to love the world is to put your confidence in the resources of the world. It is to trust man or yourself rather than God as your source of income.

On the other hand, according to John 15:4 & 5 "Remain in me and I will remain in you. No branch can bear fruit by itself; it must remain in the Vine. Neither can you bear fruit unless you remain in me. I am the vine; you are the branches. If a man remains in me and I in him, he will bear much fruit; apart from me you can do nothing."

To remain in God is to cleave to Him. It is to pray to Him continually, obey Him and to love Him and others as you love yourself. The result of doing what He asks of you is to bear much fruit for His glory.

➢ According to I John 2:15 why does God not want you to love the world or the things in it?

___

➢ What does it mean to love the things in the world?

___

➢ According to John 15:4 what are you to do?

___

➢ What is the result of remaining in God according to John 15:5?

___

DAY 41

A friend is someone who loves, sacrifices their life for another, listens and is available to help when necessary. According to Proverbs 17:17 it says, "A friend love at all times and is born, as is a brother for adversity."

There can be times of difficulty. A friend will sit with you. A friend will give themselves in service to be there in time of adversity. A friend will pray with you seeking God to heal or intervene in your time of need. A friend will laugh and rejoice with you bringing encouragement and hope to your situation.

The greatest friend is Jesus. According to John 15:13 it states, "No one has greater love [no one has shown stronger affection] than to lay down (give up) his own life for his friends."

Jesus laid down his life for all of us. He demonstrated love continually. He obeyed God the Father. He prays for us. He served us. According to Matthew 20:28 it states, "Just as the Son of Man came not to be waited on but to serve, and to give His life as a ransom for many [the price paid to set them [free].

Jesus calls His disciples and those who follow after and obey Him they are His friends. According to John 15:14 & 15 it states, "You are My friends, if you keep on doing the things which I command you to do. I do not call you servants (slaves) any longer, for the servant does not know what his master is doing (working out). But I have called you My friends, because I have made known to you everything that I have heard from My Father. [I have revealed to you everything that I have learned from Him].

What a privilege to be called a friend of God and Jesus. He allows us to spend time with Him in prayer and studying and applying the Word to our situation. He allows us to be

close to Him by listening thus being His friend. He reveals secrets to those that abide and spend time with Him who is the greatest friend. Thereby, being a friend who loves like Jesus.

➢ What is a friend?
_____
_____
_____
_____

➢ Who is the greatest friend and why?
_____
_____
_____
_____

➢ What does John 15:14 & 15 say?
_____
_____
_____
_____

➢ How have you been a friend to others?
_____
_____
_____
_____

➢ How have you been a friend of Jesus?
_____
_____
_____

DAY 42

Esther was an orphan raised by Mordecai a Godly Jewish man.

Esther found favor with King Ahasuerus. She was loved by him. A royal crown was placed upon her head becoming Queen. Esther 2:18 states, "Then the king gave a great feast for all his princes and his servants, Esther's feast; and he gave a holiday [or a lessening of taxes] to the provinces and gave gifts in keeping with the generosity of the king."

King Ahasuerus promoted Haman to set his seat above all the princes. The servants of King Ahasuerus bowed down to Haman. Mordecai told Haman his nationality that He is a Jew. After this Haman sought to destroy all the Jews. He put it in writing and published it.

According to Esther 4:1 it states, "Now when Mordecai learned all that was done, [he] rent his clothes and put on sackcloth with ashes and went out into the midst of the city and cried with a loud and bitter cry.

Then Esther 4:7 says, "And Mordecai told him of all that had happened to him, and the exact sum of money that Haman had promised to pay to the king's treasuries for the Jews to be destroyed.

Then Mordecai put out a written decree to destroy Haman which was given out in Shushan.

He showed it to Esther and explained it to her. Mordecai charged her to go to the king, make supplication to him, and plead with him for the lives of her people according to Esther 4:8. Esther then proclaimed a fast for three days, "Then I will go to the king though it is against the law; and if I perish, I perish. So Mordecai went away and did all that Esther had commanded him." According to Esther 4:16,17.

Then on the last day of the fast Esther wore her royal robes. She stood in the inner court of the king's palace place opposite his throne room. The king gave her the golden scepter that was in his hand. Esther came close and touched the tip of the scepter. Then the king asked Esther, "What is your request?" It was given to her and half the kingdom.

Esther replied, "If it seems good to the king, let the king and Haman come this day to the dinner that I have prepared for the king" according to Esther 5:3 & 4 & 6.

Henceforth," the king and Haman came to the dinner that Esther had prepared."

According to Esther 5:11 Haman recounted to them the glory of his riches, the abundance of his ten sons, all the things in which the king had promoted him and how he had advanced him above the princes and servants of the king.

Then Haman told his wife and friends that Esther made the dinner only for me.

Then in verse 13 it states, yet all this benefits me nothing as long as I see Mordecai the Jew sitting at the king's gate. In verse 14 it goes on to say, "Zeresh the wife of Haman and all his friends said to him, "Let some gallows be made, fifty cubits high and in the morning speak to the king that Mordecai may be hanged on it; then you go in merrily with the king to the dinner. And the thing pleased Haman, and he caused the gallows to be made."

In Esther 7:3 & 4 it states, "Then Queen Esther said, "O king and if it pleases the king, let my life be given me at my petition and my people at my request. For we are sold, I am my people, to be destroyed, slain and wiped out of existence! But if we had been sold for bondmen and bondwomen I would have held my tongue for our affliction is not to be compared with the damage this will do to the king. According to Esther 7:8-10 it continues by saying, then when the king returned out of the palace garden into the place of the drinking of wine, Haman was falling upon the couch where Esther was. Then the king, will he even forcibly assault the queen in my presence, in my own palace? As king spoke the words, [the servants] covered Haman's face. Then the gallows of fifty cubits' high which Haman had made for Mordecai, whose warning saved the king, stands at the house of Haman. And the king said, "Hang him on it!" So they hanged Haman on the gallows that he had prepared for Mordecai."

After this Esther asked that the letters written to destroy the Jews be reversed.

Then, the king granted the Jews to gather all the spoil from their enemies.

According to Esther 8:15 & 16, Mordecai went forth from the presence of the king in royal apparel of blue and white, with a great crown of gold and with a robe of fine linen and purple; and the city of Shushan shouted and rejoiced. The Jews had light and gladness and joy and honor.

Mordecai refused to love Haman and his ways of controlling. Rather, He stayed and honored God of Abraham, Issac and Jacob.

His love was devoted to being a Godly man to look after Esther and pray and fast for the people along with Esther.

Whenever you honor and obey God loving Him and others He intervenes on behalf of those who are being threatened and could have lost their life due to an evil man that was angry with Mordecai.

God's wisdom and love came through Esther's prayers and service to king Ahasuerus and her people. Esther risked her life to save Mordecai and the Jewish people.

The result of her love gave the Jewish people of Shushan great rejoicing in God. God gave them much spoils from their enemies.

➢ Who was Mordecai?

_____
_____
_____
_____

➢ Who was Esther?

_____
_____
_____
_____

➢ How did Esther demonstrate love for the Jewish people of Shushan?

_____
_____
_____
_____

➢ What happens when you choose God's wisdom and love to solve a problem?

_____
_____
_____
_____

➤ How did God speak to you about loving God and others through Esther's or Mordecai's life?

_____
_____
_____
_____
_____

DAY 43

Singing is a means of expressing your love for God and others.

In the book of Song of Solomon 2:4 it states, *"He has taken me to the banquet hall, and his banner over me is love."*

A banquet hall is a place for fellowship and to eat food and drink beverages. A food that many enjoy eating is Lasagna with a green salad. Whenever you go out to an Italian restaurant it is decorated with red and white table cloths. There are candles as lighting. This brings a warm and uplifting atmosphere.

Even still this is wonderful, but God's love is over us like a banner. This implies he celebrates and protects us. A banner identifies who you belong to. According to Exodus 17:15 & 16 it states, *"And Moses built an altar and called the name of it, The Lord is my Banner; And he said, because theirs is a hand against the throne of the Lord will have war with Amalek from generation to generation."*

Another aspect of God's love is that He quiets us, with His love. It states in Zephaniah 3:17, *"The Lord is with you, He is mighty to save. He will take great delight in you, He will quiet you with his love, He will rejoice over you with singing."*

In God's love He also takes pleasure in you and you can sing to Him and He sings over you as well. According to Song of Solomon 8:7 it states, *"Many waters cannot quench love; rivers cannot wash it away."*

According to Jeremiah 31:3 it says, *"I have loved you with an everlasting love; I have drawn you with loving-kindness'."*

Therefore, receive His love through singing, a Banner of Love and His quieting love. Nothing will ever quench His love for you for it is everlasting.

➢ According to Song of Solomon 2:4 what does it say about love?

➢ What does the Lord is my Banner mean according to Exodus 17:8-16?

➢ According to Zephaniah 3:17 what does the Lord do?

➢ Can anything quench you from God's love according to Song of Solomon 8:7?

➢ What does Jeremiah 31:3 say? How did God speak to you about His love in this lesson?

_____
_____
_____
_____
_____
_____

DAY 44

Psalm 91 tells us where the best place to be is upon this earth. It is to remain in the secret place of the Most High. He will keep you stable and confident in Him. His shadow of the Almighty has power that no foe can withstand.

God is our Refuge and Fortress. You can trust Him and look to Him to bring deliverance from entrapment of the enemy and from deadly pestilence. He covers you in His wings of protection. He is truthful, trustworthy and faithful. He is a shield and a buckler.

Fear shall not grip you in the night time. No evil plots and slanders of the wicked that may fly by day, or even pestilence that may come in the dark, not even a plague that may come to destroy at noontime. It cannot come near you. A thousand will fall at your side. As well as ten thousand at your right hand. You will observe or see with your eyes and see the punishment of the wicked because you remained in the Lord your Refuge and He became your dwelling place.

Therefore, no evil will befall you, nor any plague or calamity comes near your home or wherever you may be.

His angels will guard and protect you by accompanying you. They will defend and preserve you in all your ways.

The angels will give you a lift of their hands, so you will not be harmed by a stone that hits your foot. You will trample on the lion and the cobra and the serpent.

"Because he loves me, says the Lord, "I will rescue him." I will protect you. You have acknowledged my name and you call upon me and I do answer you. In time of trouble, I will manifest to you my salvation."

This psalm is God's will to you when you make Him Your dwelling place. He protects you and keeps you confident in Him. He loves you and you love Him. Therefore, you will see the deliverance of the Lord. He answers your prayers. He will satisfy you with long life as you remain in Him as your refuge.

➤ Where is the best place to be upon the earth according to Psalm 91:1?

➤ What does God promise to do according to Psalm 91:3?

➤ According to Psalm 91:5-7 why should you not be fearful?

➤ According to Psalm 91:11 & 12 what does God do?

➢ Write down God's I will's in Psalm 91.

_____
_____
_____
_____
_____

➢ How did God speak to you through Psalm 91?

_____
_____
_____
_____
_____

DAY 45

In John 6:4-13 Jesus is with his disciples. Passover is approaching. Jesus speaks to Philip, *"Where shall we buy bread for these people to eat?" Jesus asks Philip to test him because He knew what God wanted him to do. Philip answered him, "Eight months' wages would not buy enough bread for each one to have a bite."*

Andrew, Simon Peter's brother spoke up, "Here is a boy with five small barley loaves and two small fish. How far will they go among this multitude?

Jesus said, "Have the people sit down." There was grass in this place so all the people obeyed and sat down.

Jesus took the loaves, gave thanks and distributed to those who were seated as much as they wanted. He did the same with the fish.

They all had plenty to eat and they gathered enough leftovers filled twelve baskets with the pieces of the five barley loaves.

Jesus demonstrates God's love to see to it that the multitude is fed, exercises faith and obeys God by giving thanks exhibiting and knowing that God's love is faithful to feed and meet the people's needs.

Jesus met their needs. He is no respecter of person's. He will meet our needs as well. Psalm 37:25 states, *"I was young and now old, yet, I have never seen the righteous forsaken or their children begging for bread."*

Therefore, Let's look up and give thanks by, *"Tasting and seeing that the Lord is good blessed is the man who takes refuge in Him. Fear the Lord, you His saints for those who fear Him lack nothing. The lions may grow weak and hungry, but those who seek the Lord lack no good thing."* Psalm 34:8-10.

➤ What was the problem in John 6:4?

_____
_____
_____
_____
_____

➤ How did Jesus solve the problem according to John 6:10-13?

_____
_____
_____
_____
_____

➤ How much was leftover according to John 6:13?

_____
_____
_____
_____
_____

➤ How did God speak to you in this lesson concerning His faithful love?

_____
_____
_____
_____
_____

DAY 46

In John 21 after Peter and some of Jesus' disciples go fishing with Jesus. They discover that without Jesus and His wisdom they couldn't catch any fish. However, whenever we follow His directions and obey them there is more than enough.

Jesus anoints and reinstates Peter after they had eaten breakfast. Jesus asks Peter, "Simon son of John, do you truly love me more than these?" Peter answers, "Yes, Lord. Jesus you know that I love you." Jesus replied, "Feed my lambs."

To feed lambs is to feed new believers and teach them to walk, live and obey Jesus in His Word and do that which Jesus did.

Again, Jesus asks Peter, do you truly love me? Peter replied, "Yes, Lord, you know that I love you." Jesus replied, "Take care of my sheep."

Jesus was asking Peter to have brotherly love for others by being a Shepherd taking care of them and by leading them to walk in the ways of Jesus.

Then Jesus asks Peter a third time, "Do you love me?" Peter was hurt because Jesus asked him the same question three times. He knew that Jesus is Lord. He knows all things. Jesus you know that I love you. Jesus said, "Feed my sheep. Jesus answering honestly told Peter that when you were young you dressed yourself and went wherever you wanted but when you are old you will stretch out your hands and someone else will dress you and lead you where you do not want to go."

Jesus was reminding Peter that he had denied Jesus three times. Therefore, Jesus reinstates Peter telling him the cost it would be when He gets old. He followed Jesus like a rock and died crucified upside down. Peter said, "he was not worthy to die just like Jesus."

There can be three stages of love. The infant stage. Take care of my own needs.

The second stage of love is to love others like a brother or sister.

Then the last stage, are you willing to risk your life and honor, obey or even Shepherd the sheep for Jesus to be the light and even die that others know that you are a disciple or a lover of Jesus?

➢ In John 21:6 what happened when they threw the net on the right side?

➢ According to John 21:15 what did Jesus ask Peter?

➢ According to John 15:17-19 why did Jesus ask Peter the love question for the third time?

➢ What did the Lord teach you in this lesson?

DAY 47

A woman who showed great love for Jesus was Mary of Bethany. According to John 11:2 it states, *"This Mary was the one who anointed the Lord with perfume and wiped His feet with her hair."*

Mary loved Jesus and demonstrated her love for Him by taking a pound of ointment of pure liquid nard. This was a rare perfume. It was expensive. She poured it onto the feet of Jesus. She wiped it with her hair. The place smelled eloquently and She felt He was worthy of such love. It came from her heart and She gave Him her best perfume. She humbled herself by bowing down and wiping Him with her hair. Hair was also considered a woman's crown of glory.

Judas' response to all of this was according to John 12:5 it states, *"Why was this perfume not sold for a year's wages for an ordinary workmen and the money given to the poor?"* Judas said this because He was a thief and cared not for the poor. According to John 12:7-9 it states Jesus' reply, *"Let her alone. It was that she should keep it for the time of My preparation for burial. [she has kept it that she might have it for the time of My embalming]. You always have the poor with you, but you do not always have Me."*

Your heart matters to Jesus. He appreciated and received Mary's expression of love for Him.

Jesus knows your motive for doing things. Judas was a thief. But, Mary was a lover of Jesus. Jesus desires us to give from an expression of love and not because of greed.

Mary and Jesus gave from a heart of love and sacrifice. Let's follow after love.

➤ According to John 11:2 what did Mary do for Jesus?
___
___
___
___
___

➤ What was the cost of her love monetarily according to John 12:5?
___
___
___
___
___

➤ What was Judas according to John 12:6?
___
___
___
___
___

➤ What was Jesus' answer after Judas' question in John 12:5?
___
___
___
___
___

MERCIFUL: A DEVOTIONAL JOURNAL

➤ What did the Lord teach you about following after love in this lesson?

_____
_____
_____
_____
_____

DAY 48

According to John 13:1 it states, *"It was just before the Passover Feast. Jesus knew that the time had come for him to leave this world and go to the Father. Having loved his own who were in the world he now showed them the full extent of His love."*

The Passover Feast was a fore shadow of what was to come. According to Exodus 12:1-16 it states they were to take a lamb for your family, one for each household. You will need to figure out how much lamb is needed according to what each person will eat. The lamb must be without defect. At twilight you must slaughter it. Then take some of the blood and apply it to the sides and tops of the door frames of the houses where they eat the lambs. Then the same night they are to eat the meat roasted over the bread made without yeast. Do not eat the meat raw or cooked in water, but roast it over the fire; the head, legs and inner parts. Do not leave any of it till morning. If there is some left burn it. This is how you are to eat it; with your cloak tucked into your belt, your sandals on, your feet and your staff in your hand. Eat it in haste; it is the Lord's Passover.

On that same night I will pass through Egypt and strike down every firstborn_ both men and animals_ and I will bring judgment on all the gods of Egypt. I am the Lord. The blood will be a sign for you on the houses where you are; and when I see the blood, I will pass over you. No destructive plague will touch you when I strike Egypt.

This is a day you are to commemorate you shall celebrate it as a festival to the Lord. It shall be celebrated as a lasting ordinance. For seven days you are to eat bread made without yeast. On the first day remove the yeast from your houses, for whoever eats anything with yeast in it from the first day through the seventh must be cut off from Israel. On the first day hold a sacred assembly and another one on the seventh day. Do not work at all on these days, except to prepare food for everyone to eat that is all you may do.

Jesus became the Passover Lamb. According to Isaiah 53:3-12 it states, *"He was despised and rejected by men, a man of sorrows and familiar with suffering. Like one from whom men hide their faces he was despised, and we esteemed him not. Surely he took up our infirmities and carried our sorrows, yet we considered him stricken by God, smitten by him and afflicted. But he was pierced for our transgressions, he was crushed for our iniquities; the punishment that brought us peace was upon him, and by his wounds we are healed. We all like sheep have gone astray, each of us has turned to his own way; and the Lord has laid on him the iniquity of us all. He was oppressed and afflicted, yet he did not open his mouth; he was led like a lamb to the slaughter, and as a sheep before her shearers is silent, so he did not open his mouth. By oppression and judgment, he was taken away. And who can speak of his descendants? For he was cut off from the land of the living; for the transgression of my people he was stricken. He was assigned a grave with the wicked, and with the rich in his death, though he had done no violence nor was any deceit in his mouth, yet it was the Lord's will to crush him and cause him to suffer and though the Lord makes his life a guilt offering, he will see his offspring and prolong his days, and the will of the Lord will prosper in his hand. After the suffering of his soul, he will see the light of life and be satisfied; by his knowledge my righteous servant will justify many, and he will bear their iniquities. Therefore, I will give him a portion among the great, and he will divide the spoils with the strong because he poured out his life unto death, and was numbered with the transgressors. For he bore the sin of many and made intercession for the transgressors."*

Jesus took our sins and they were laid upon Him. This was the greatest demonstration of love. He was beaten, mocked, and like a lamb was slaughtered and he did no sin. He was without blemish or the spotless Lamb of God. He bled on the cross and at twilight He was on the cross to die for my sin and the world's sin. He felt sorrow, much pain and did not say a word except for Father, forgive them, for they do not know what they do.

His act of love compels me to devote my life and my all because of His amazing love.

➢ According to Exodus 12 what were the people to do in their home?
_____
_____
_____
_____
_____

➢ Write out Isaiah 53:6.
_____
_____
_____
_____
_____

➢ How did Jesus meet the will of God according to Isaiah 53:10 & 11?
_____
_____
_____
_____
_____

➢ How did the Lord Jesus reveal His love to you in this lesson?
_____
_____
_____
_____

DAY 49

John 13:4-17 it tells us Jesus, after He had finished eating, took off his outer clothing and wrapped a towel around his waist. After that, he poured water into a basin and began to wash his disciples' feet drying them with the towel that was wrapped around him.

Jesus came to Simon Peter, who said to him, "Lord are you going to wash my feet?" Jesus answered Peter by saying, "You do not realize now what I am doing, but later you will understand." Peter said, "No you will never wash my feet,"

Jesus answered, "Unless I wash you, you have no part with me." Then, Lord, Simon Peter replied, "not just my feet but my hands and my head as well." Jesus answered, "A person who has had a bath needs only to wash his feet his whole body is clean. And you are clean, though not everyone of you." For he knew who would betray him, and that was why he said not every one was clean.

When he had finished washing their feet, he put on his clothes and returned to his place. Jesus asks them, "Do you understand what I have done for you?" You call me Teacher and Lord, and rightly so, for that is what I am. Now that I, your Lord and Teacher, have washed your feet you also should wash one another's feet. I tell you the truth, no servant is greater than his master, nor is a messenger greater than the one who sent him. Now that you know these things you will be blessed if you do them."

Jesus sets the example of love by demonstrating to his disciples' humility by cleaning the disciple's feet. They wore sandals and walked everywhere they traveled. They cleaned the animals, the stables, the barns had animal feces and the roads were dusty or muddy etc. Also, Jesus was Lord and Teacher and no one is greater than him or your disciple or yourself. We are exercising God's love by serving in this way. Jesus ends his teaching by saying, Blessed are you by doing these things.

➢ Why according to John 13:8 did Jesus wash the disciple's feet?

___

➢ How did Jesus answer Simon Peter's question according to John 13:10?

___

➢ Why wash one another's feet according to John 13:12-16?

___

➢ Write out John 13:17.

___

MERCIFUL: A DEVOTIONAL JOURNAL | 119

➤ How did the Lord speak to you in this lesson?

_____
_____
_____
_____
_____

DAY 50

According to John 19:38-42 it states, "Later, 'Joseph of Arimathea asked Pilate for the body of Jesus. Now Joseph was a disciple of Jesus, but secretly because he feared the Jews. With Pilate's permission, he came and took the body away. He was accompanied by Nicodemus, the man who earlier had visited Jesus at night. Nicodemus brought a mixture of myrrh and aloes, about 75 pounds. Taking Jesus' body, the two of them wrapped it, with the spices, in strips of linen. This was in accordance with Jewish burial customs. At the place where Jesus was crucified, there was a garden, and in the garden a new tomb, in which no one had ever been laid. Because it was the Jewish day of preparation and since the tomb was nearby, they laid Jesus there.

Joseph of Arimathea got permission by Pilate for the body of Jesus to be taken away. He was accompanied by Nicodemus.

Joseph of Arimathea was a follower of Jesus. Nicodemus was a Pharisee and a member of the Jewish ruling council. Nicodemus in John 3:3 is taught by Jesus and saw the miracles that Jesus did.

Jesus tells Nicodemus You must be born again. Jesus tells him in John 3:5 & 6, *"I tell you the truth, no one can enter the Kingdom of God unless he is born of water and Spirit. Flesh gives birth to flesh, but the Spirit gives birth to spirit."*

It is implied that even though Jesus is buried and in a tomb that God wanted a message sent that of salvation.

You must be born again. Again receiving this message is love. Joseph of Arimathea a man who showed his love for Jesus by being there to bury Jesus. Nicodemus also loved Jesus. Another message is Joseph of Arimathea and Nicodemus were serving and showing love to Jesus practically by being at the burial and by bringing spices of 75 pounds as was the custom Thereby, not allowing fear of the Jews to stop them from being apart of the burial of Jesus.

➢ According to John 19:38 who asked Pilate for the body of Jesus?

➢ Who accompanied Joseph of Arimathea?

➢ What was implied by Nicodemus being at the burial? John 3:3, 5 & 6.

➢ How did the Lord speak to you in this lesson?

DAY 51

In Matthew 28:1-10 it is the account of the resurrection of Jesus.

"After the Sabbath, at dawn on the first day of the week, Mary Magdalene and the other Mary went to look at the tomb.

There was a violent earthquake, for an angel of the Lord came down from heaven and going to the tomb, rolled back the stone and sat on it. His appearance was like lightning and his clothes were white as snow. The guards were so afraid of him that they shook and became like dead men.

The angel said to the women, "Do not be afraid, for I know that you are looking for Jesus who was crucified. He is not here; he has risen, just as he said. Come and see the place where he lay. Then, go quickly and tell his disciples: He has risen from the dead and is going ahead of you into Galilee. There you will see him.' Now I have told you." So the women hurried away from the tomb, afraid yet filled with joy, and ran to tell his disciples. Suddenly, Jesus met them. "Greetings," He said. They came to Him clasped His feet and worshiped Him. Then Jesus said to them, "Do not be afraid. Go and tell my brothers to go to Galilee; there they will see me."

It was approximately 6a.m. on a Sunday Mary Magdalene and the other Mary go to the tomb where Jesus was laid. There was plenty of rocking and shaking for there was an earthquake. An angel of the Lord came and rolled back the stone and sat down on it. The angel speaks to the women and tells them to not be frightened. Jesus who was crucified who you are looking for has risen from the tomb. Go quickly and tell my disciples that He has risen from the dead.

Then the women had fear mixed with great joy running to tell the disciples. Suddenly, Jesus appears to them saying,

"Greetings." They all came to Jesus and held His feet and worshiped Him.

We as believers join in song, "Up From the Grave He Arose with a Mighty Triumph over His foes."

The women and others devoted their love to Jesus by going to the tomb of Jesus. Jesus revealed His love for the women and others by saying, "Greetings" and showing to them I am alive and well. He loved them and they loved Him too by worshiping a risen Lord and Savior.

➢ According to Matthew 28:1 who came to see the tomb first?

___

➢ According to Matthew 28:2 & 3 what happened and who came to Mary Magdalene and the other Mary?

___

➢ According to Matthew 28:8 & 9 what happened?

___

➢ How did the Lord speak to you about love in this lesson?

___

DAY 52

An expression of love is to pray. Prayer gives access to heaven's agenda for your life, others and yields to God. Prayer shows how big He is. Nothing is impossible with God.

Jesus expresses His love in John 17:15-19 it states, *"My prayer is not that you take them out of the world but that you protect them from the evil one. They are not of the world, even as I am not of it. Sanctify them by the truth your word is truth. As you sent me into the world. I have sent them into the world. For them I sanctify myself, that they too may be truly sanctified."*

Jesus desires us to be set apart from the world. He set the example, and as believers prays that we would follow the truth and stand on God's word of truth.

In addition, John 17:20-25 states, *"My prayer is not for them alone. I pray also for those who will believe in me through their message, that all of them may be one. Father, just as you are in me and I am in you. May they also be in us so that the world may believe that you have sent me. I have given them the glory that you gave me, that they may be one as we are one: I in them and you in me. May they be brought to complete unity to let the world know that you sent me and have loved them even as you have loved me.*

Father, I want those you have given me to be with me where I am and to see my glory, the glory you have given me because you loved me before the creation of the world.

Righteous Father, though the world does not know you, I know you and they know that you have sent me. I have made you known to them, and will continue to make you known in order that the love you have for me may be in them."

In today's world an example of this has been a virus that has spread all over the world.

The doctors, nurses, President Trump, Vice President Pence and the president's task force have been instruments of unity. The governors of the states and the mayors have demonstrated love with unity. Their focus has been on loving others and working together with the community to make masks and instruct the people to wash their hands and practice safe distancing.

Also food banks have worked together in love to see that people's need of food is given to families and those such as seniors who are not able to get the food for themselves, others are delivering food to them.

President Trump also has prayed for everyone and continues to demonstrate love for the country. He was given wisdom by God to give out stimulus package to aid people, families and small businesses to demonstrate love by seeing that people have financial means during this virus test.

During this virus test and staying at home has caused me to draw closer to God. He has been revealing His love to me, my husband and my family. He continues to talk to me through his word and prayer. He told me that Jesus is real. He gives me His prayers to pray for those that are going through this test of the virus. He reminds me that He wears the Victor's Crown. He conquered death, sickness and arose from the dead. When you receive Him and pray with Him you too are victorious.

May we too be in unity and demonstrate God's love to the world for His glory.

➤ According to John 17:15-19 what two things does Jesus pray?

➤ According to John 17:20-25 what and who is Jesus praying for?

➤ How did God speak to you about His love in this lesson?

DAY 53

Jesus in Matthew 6:19-21, 24 states, *"Do not store up for yourselves treasures on earth, where moth and rust destroy and where thieves break in and steal. But store up for yourselves treasures in heaven, where moth and rust do not destroy, and where thieves do not break in and steal. For where your treasure is there your heart will be also.*

No one can serve two masters, either he will hate the one and love the other, or he will be devoted to the one and despise the other. You cannot serve both God and money."

Jesus exhorts us to not serve or love money more than you love God. He tells us that by storing things or riches on the earth that they are not lasting. It brings with it thieves that can break in and steal. This is an indicator where your heart lies. You cannot love God and money. God needs to be first otherwise this is idolatry.

Jesus in Matthew 6:25-33 states, *"Therefore I tell you, do not worry about your life, what you will eat or drink; or about your body, what you will wear. Is not life, more important than food, and the body more important than clothes? Look at the birds of the air; they do not sow or reap or store away in barns, and yet your heavenly Father feeds them. Are you not much more valuable than they? Who of you by worrying can add a single hour to his life?*

And why do you worry about clothes? See how the lilies of the field grow. They do not labor or spin. Yet I tell you that not even Solomon in all his splendor was dressed like one of these. If that is how God clothes the grass of the field, which is here today and tomorrow is thrown into the fire, will he not much more clothe you, O you of little faith? So do not worry, saying, 'What shall we eat?' or 'What shall we drink?' or 'What shall we wear?' For the pagans run after all these things, and your heavenly Father knows that you need them. But seek first his Kingdom and His righteousness, and all these things will be given to you as well. Therefore, do not worry about tomorrow, for tomorrow will worry about itself. Each day has enough trouble of its own."

God is a loving heavenly Father who knows human nature can be tempted to worry about what to eat, drink or wear as clothing. He tells us a word picture and uses the birds of the air as an example of His care and love. We are more cherished than the birds and even Solomon in all his splendor. Therefore, know that God loves you, put Him first, do his right ways, honor Him and the Kingdom of God and all these things will be supplied by Him.

In I Timothy 6:6-10a it states, *"But godliness with contentment is great gain. For we brought nothing into the world, and we can take nothing out of it. But if we have food and clothing, we will be content with that. People who want to get rich fall into temptation and a trap and into many foolish and harmful desires that plunge men into ruin and destruction. For the love of money is a root of all kinds of evil."*

To be content is to be thankful for the provision of our loving heavenly Father. He is our source and He knows our needs before we even ask for them. Therefore, do not fall into the snare of the love of money. Money is a means and God is supreme, good, loving, faithful and beautiful. Keep seeking Him first and His Kingdom giving Him first place in your heart.

- According to Matthew 6:19 & 20 what can happen if you store up earthly treasure for yourself?

- Write out Matthew 6:20 & 21.

- According to Matthew 6:25-33 why does God say, "Do not worry?"

- According to Matthew 6:33 what does God instruct us to do?

➤ According to I Timothy 6:6 what matters most concerning your heart and attitude?

_____
_____
_____
_____
_____

➤ How did God speak to you in this lesson?

_____
_____
_____
_____
_____

DAY 54

Paul went through many hardships. He was in prison. He was ship wrecked on the Island of Malta. The people of Malta showed Paul unusual kindness by kindling a fire to keep them warm. The weather was cold and rainy. They embraced them. According to Acts 28:3 & 5 it states, *"Paul had gathered a bundle of sticks, and he was laying them on the fire when a viper crawled out because of the heat and fastened itself on his hand. Then Paul shook off the small creature into the fire and suffered no evil effects."*

The people of Malta saw God in Paul especially after seeing that Paul had no bad repercussions from being bit by the vipor.

Publius received Paul and those that were with him. They gave them love through showing them hospitality for three days.

Paul showed God's love to Publius' father, praying and by laying hands on him and He was healed from a fever and dysentery.

Acts 28:9 & 10 states, *"After this had occurred, the other people on the island who had diseases also kept coming and were cured. They showed us every respect and presented many gifts to us, honoring us with many honors; and put on [board our ship] everything we needed."*

There can be hardships in life. Yet, according to Romans 8:28 God uses everything to the good to those who love God and are called according to His purpose. God's love to you and to those whom you may be ministering to through you. He used God's gift of healing through Paul to open up an Island that needed to experience God's healing love. The result was that God demonstrated back to Paul and those on the ship hospitality for three days. He also made sure all their needs were met through Publius.

Therefore, no matter what you may be going through God loves and knows our needs. He uses our gifts to demonstrate His love to those in our lives.

➢ According to Acts 28:3 & 5 what happened?

_____
_____
_____
_____

➢ According to Acts 28:8 & 9 what did God do through

_____
_____
_____
_____

➢ Paul? According to Acts 28:10 how did Publius honor Paul?

_____
_____
_____
_____

➢ How will you let God demonstrate His love through you by using your gifts?

_____
_____
_____
_____

DAY 55

In the book of Ephesians Paul prays for the believers of Ephesus. Ephesians 1:15-23 states, "For this reason, because I have heard of your faith in the Lord Jesus and your love toward all the saints. I do not cease to give thanks for you, making mention of you in my prayers. [For I always pray to] the God of our Lord Jesus Christ, the Father glory, that He may grant you a spirit of wisdom and revelation [of insight into mysteries and secrets] in the [deep and intimate] knowledge of Him, by having the eyes of your heart flooded with light, so that you can know and understand the hope to which He has called you, and how rich is His glorious inheritance in the saints. And [so that you can know and understand] what is the immeasurable and unlimited and surpassing greatness of His power in and for us who believe, as demonstrated in the working of His mighty strength, which He exerted in Christ when He raised Him from the dead and seated Him at His right hand in the heavenly places. Far above all rule and authority and power and dominion and every name that is named, not only in this age and in this world, but also in the age and the world which are to come. And He has put all things under His feet and his appointed Him the universal and Supreme Head of the church. Which is His body, the fullness of Him who fills all in all [for in that body lives the full measure of Him who makes everything complete, and who fills everything everywhere with Himself].

As believers Paul's prayer is important to pray in our own lives. Everyday we need the Spirit of wisdom and revelation to know Jesus better. Not only do we need wisdom and revelation to know Jesus but as believers we need it to make Godly decisions to obey Him. Thereby, to live our lives so He is seen and glorified in our lives. It takes His light in our heart to know the hope to which we have been called.

His riches bring spiritual wealth to our soul to walk worthy of His calling. Spending daily time with Jesus removes emotional, physical and even psychological hindrances to our walk with Him. We experience His love and His power of strength which was exercised in Jesus when He was raised from the dead. Then He was seated at the right hand of God in the heavenly realm. God placed everything under His feet. Jesus is the head of everything including us as the church.

Therefore, like Paul lets allow the Holy Spirit to have His way in our lives. Then Jesus will be known to the world as the head exemplifying the love and light to the world.

➢ According to Ephesians 1:15 why is Paul praying?

➢ What three things does Paul pray concern believer's?

➢ According to Ephesians 1:19, 20 explain Jesus' power?

➢ Who heads the church according to Ephesians 1:22,23? How did the Lord speak to you through this lesson?

DAY 56

Paul in Ephesians 3:14-20 prays for the believers of Ephesus. He prays, *"For this reason seeing the greatness of this plan by which you are built together in Christ, I bow my knees before the Father of our Lord Jesus Christ, for whom every family in heaven and on earth is named [that Father from whom all fatherhood takes its title and derives its name]. May He grant you out of the rich treasury of His glory to be strengthened and reinforced with mighty power in the inner man by the [Holy] Spirit [Himself indwelling your innermost being and personality]. May Christ through your faith [actually] dwell (settle down, abide, make His permanent home) in your hearts! May you be rooted deep in love and founded securely on love, that you may have the power and be strong to apprehend and grasp with all the saints [God's devoted people the experience of that love] what is the breadth and length and height and depth[of it]; [that you may really come] to know [practically, through experience for yourselves] the love of Christ, which far surpasses mere knowledge [without experience]; that you may be filled [through all your being] unto all the fullness of God [may have the richest measure of the divine Presence, and become a body wholly filled and flooded with God Himself]! Now to Him who, by (in consequence of the [action of His] power that is at work within us, is able to [carry out His purpose and] do superabundantly, far over and above all that we [dare] ask or think [infinitely beyond our highest prayers, desires, thoughts, hopes, or dreams] – To Him be glory in the church and in Christ Jesus throughout all generations forever and ever. Amen."*

Paul prays for the church of Ephesus as well as includes every believer that Father God would bestow his rich treasury of His glory. May you be strengthened and be daily reinforced with the Holy Spirit's mighty power inwardly to the point that it permanents you and your personality. May you be filled with faith allowing the Spirit of God to dwell in you making Him right at home in your heart. May His love go deep. May you be secure in His love. Thereby, having His power and His strength to apprehend and lay hold of with all God's devoted believers, the experience of His love what is the breadth, length, height and depth of His love now and always. Paul continues to ask God to give believers practical experiences that exceed knowledge thereby, allowing the Spirit of God to lead, guide, direct, speak, and love indwelling you completely. Thereby, He is able to do immeasurable, beyond what you may ask, think or imagine according to His power indwelling inside of you. May God receive all the glory now and forevermore in us. Amen.

➢ According to Ephesians 3:16 how are you strengthened?

➢ What does Paul ask God to do according to Ephesians 3:17- 19?

➢ Write out Ephesians 3:20?

➢ Look at Day 55 Paul prays for believers how is Ephesians 1:15-21 similar? How is it different from Ephesians 3:14- 20?

➤ How did the Spirit of God speak to you about His love in this lesson?

_____
_____
_____
_____

DAY 57

Paul a man of prayer extends his prayers to Philippi. His prayer is stated in Philippians 1:9-11, *"I pray that your love may abound yet more and more and extend to its fullest development in knowledge and all keen insight [that your love may display itself in greater depth of acquaintance and more comprehensive discernment], So that you may surely learn to sense what is vital, and approve and prize what is excellent and of real value [recognizing the highest and the best, and distinguishing the moral differences], and that you may be untainted and pure and unerring and blameless [so that with hearts sincere and certain and unsullied, you may approach] the day of Christ [not stumbling nor causing others to stumble]. May you abound in and be filled with the fruits of righteousness (of right standing with God and right doing) which come through Jesus Christ (the Anointed One), to the honor and praise of God [that His glory may be both manifested and recognized]."*

Paul is praying while in prison. He prays that your love grows to the point of rich knowledge and discernment. He prays that your love is manifested by displaying integrity, Godly right living and purity until the day of Christ. May Jesus receive all the glory and praise of God.

According to Philippians 3:7-11 it states, *"But whatever was to my profit I now consider loss for the sake of Christ. What is more, I consider everything a loss compared to the surpassing greatness of knowing Christ Jesus my Lord, for whose sake I have lost all things. I consider them rubbish that I may gain Christ and be found in him, not having a righteousness of my own that comes from the law, but that which is through faith in Christ- the righteousness that comes from God and by faith. I want to know Christ and the fellowship of sharing in his sufferings, becoming like him in his death, and so, somehow, to attain to the resurrection from the dead."* Christ is Lord! May He be magnified, supreme and number one in our lives. May we honor Him no matter what situation we may be in. May we fellowship with Christ receiving His love to live the life He desires for us. Even when we suffer He suffered and died for us. Therefore, let's continue to lay down our lives for His glory. May we get to know Him and receive His resurrection of life to live our lives as He destined and created for us to live.

➢ What does Paul pray in Philippians 1:9?

➢ According to Philippians 1:10 what does Paul pray?

➢ According to Philippians 1:11 what does Paul ask that God does?

➢ According to Philippians 3:10 how does Paul want to know Christ? How did God speak to you through this lesson?

DAY 58

In the book of Philippians Paul exhorts believers in chapter 4:6-8 it states, *"Do not fret or have any anxiety about anything, but in circumstance and in everything by prayer and petition (definite requests), with thanksgiving, continue to make your wants known to God. And God's peace [shall be yours, that tranquil state of a soul assured of its salvation through Christ, and so fearing nothing from God and being content with its earthly lot of whatever sort that is, that peace] which transcends all understanding shall garrison and mount guard over your hearts and minds in Christ Jesus. For the rest, brethren, whatever is true, whatever is worthy of reverence and is honorable and seemly, whatever is just, whatever is pure, whatever is lovely and lovable, whatever is kind and winsome and gracious, if there is any virtue and excellence, if there is anything worthy of praise, think on and weigh and take account of these things [fix your minds on them]."*

Hence from the other letters that Paul has written concerning prayer here is explicit directions from God to not worry or have anxiety about anything. In today's world commit the Corona Virus to Jesus and pray. Do not concern yourself about any job loss or what you will eat. Look to Jesus laying everything down. Believe God's word. *"He shall supply all your need according to His riches in glory by Christ Jesus our Lord." Philippians 4:19.*

He is our peace. *"He will keep you in perfect peace whose mind is stayed on thee." Isaiah 26:3.*

Be thankful and content that God is working, He sees, He cares, He loves and He is victorious over everything. Allow God's word to be your strength and to be your life force receiving His promise for your situation.

Paul exhorts us to think upon the truth, the noble, the right, whatever is pure and lovely. Think about the goodness of God. He is always faithful and He is trustworthy. Therefore, do not worry, but rejoice in the Lord; always! Philippians 4:4.

➢ According to Philippians 4:6 what are we to do?

___

➢ According to Philippians 4:7 explain what is promised?

___

➢ Write out Philippians 4:8.

___

➢ How did God speak to you through this lesson?

___

DAY 59

Paul's letter written to Timothy, Philemon, Sister Apphia and a fellow soldier in Christ Jesus. Also to the believers who meet in their home.

Philemon 3-7 states, *"Grace to you and peace from God our Father and the Lord Jesus Christ. I always thank my God as I remember you in my prayers, because hear about your faith in the Lord Jesus and your love for all the saints. I pray that you may be active in sharing your faith, so that you will have a full understanding of every good thing we have in Christ. Your love has given me great joy and encouragement, because you, brother, have refreshed the hearts of the saints."*

God's love is being displayed through Philemon a worker for Christ. His love operates through a home church. Paul expresses appreciation to those who are a part of this home church. Paul also expresses to Philemon that "your love has given me great joy and encouragement, because you, brother, have refreshed the hearts of the saints."

In today's world we fellowship through social media. We have various groups of people some small others larger who fellowship and express their thoughts and love for each other.

In Hebrews 10:24 & 25 it states, *"And let us consider how we may spur one another on toward love and good deeds. Let us not give up meeting together, as some are in the habit of doing, but let us encourage one another- and all the more as you see the Day approaching."*

An expression of love comes through encouraging words. It also comes by fellowshipping together and learning together about God's word. It also comes through praying together and by serving each other in love.

The Lord is coming soon!

➢ According to Philemon 7 what does Paul mention to Philemon?

➢ How has social media allowed you to fellowship with other believers?

➢ Write out Hebrews 10:24 & 25?

➢ How did the Lord speak to you in this lesson?

DAY 60

Peter too was a man of prayer. He suffered in the flesh and we will too. He exhorts us to please God. According to I Peter 4:1 & 2 it states, *"Therefore, since Christ suffered in his body, arm yourselves also with the same attitude, because he who has suffered in his body is done with sin, as a result, he does not live the rest of his earthly life for evil human desires, but rather for the will of God."*

According to I Peter 4:7-11 it states, *"The end of all things is near. Therefore be clear minded and self-controlled. So that you can pray. Above all, love each other deeply, because love covers over a multitude of sins. Offer hospitality to one another without grumbling. Each one should use whatever gift he has received to serve others, faithfully administering God's grace in its various forms. If anyone speaks, he should do it as one speaking the very words of God. If anyone serves, he should do it with the strength God provides, so that in all things God may be praised through Jesus Christ. To Him be the glory and the power for ever and ever. Amen."*

The will of God is to be sound minded exercising self-discipline; always praying with God's love. God's love is deep. It does not keep account of record of wrongs. It offers hospitality without complaining. Serving with God's love with your gift that needs to be done faithfully and with God's grace. Whenever you are speaking speak God's loving words. When serving do it with God's strength. He will be praised through Jesus Christ. May He be glorified and His power be manifested always. Amen.

Jude warns us as believers that in the last days there will be people who seek to gratify themselves and not living Godly lives.

On the other hand, Jude writes, "But you, dear friends, build yourselves up in your most holy faith and pray in the Holy Spirit. Keep yourselves in God's love as you wait for the mercy of our Lord Jesus Christ to bring you to eternal life."

"Be merciful to those who doubt; snatch others from the fire and save them; to others show mercy, mixed with fear – hating even the clothing stained by corrupted flesh." "To

Him who is able to keep you from falling and to present you before His glorious presence without fault and with great joy- to the only God our Savior be glory, majesty, power and authority, through Jesus Christ our Lord, before all ages, now and forevermore! Amen."

In Peter's letter he focuses on us demonstrating God's Character. His love without hypocrisy. His love without complaining. Our strength comes through Christ motivated by love.

But in Jude he writes that you build yourself up by yielding to God's Holy faith by praying in the Holy Spirit. Stay in love for God and others displaying the mercy of the Lord Jesus Christ until he takes you home to glory.

Allow your light to shine so that others that do not believe may see God's love in you. Thereby, led them to the saving grace of the Lord Jesus.

May He keep you from falling. May He present you before His glorious presence blameless and with great joy. Glory, majesty, power and authority to God our Savior and Lord for all times and forevermore! Amen.

➢ According to I Peter 4:1 & 2 what are you to do?

➢ According to I Peter 4:7-11 name the five things we are asked to do in light of the end being near?

➢ According to Jude 20-25 how do we build up ourselves in our Most Holy Faith?

➢ How did the Lord speak to you in this lesson?

DAY 61

There is a great exchange mentioned in the Bible. It is in Isaiah 61 and it states, "The Spirit of the Sovereign Lord is on me, because the Lord has anointed me to preach good news to the poor. He has sent me to bind up the brokenhearted, to proclaim freedom for the captives and captives and release from darkness for the prisoners, to proclaim the year of the Lord's favor and the day of vengeance of our God, to comfort all who mourn, and provide for those who grieve in Zion- to bestow on them a crown of beauty instead of ashes, the oil of gladness instead of mourning and a garment of praise instead of a Spirit of despair. They will be called oaks of righteousness a planting of the Lord for the display of His splendor. They will rebuild the ancient ruins and restore the places long devastated; they will renew the ruined cities that have been devastated for generations. Aliens will shepherd your flocks; foreigners will work your fields and vineyards. And you will be called priests of the Lord, you will be named ministers of our God. You will feed on the wealth of nations, and in their riches you will boast. Instead of their shame my people will receive a double portion, and instead of disgrace they will rejoice in their inheritance; and so they will inherit a double portion in their land and everlasting joy will be theirs. For I, the Lord, love justice; I hate robbery and iniquity. In my faithfulness I will reward them and make an everlasting covenant with them. Their descendants will be known among the nations and their offspring among the peoples. All who see them will acknowledge that they are a people the Lord has blessed.

I delight greatly in the Lord; my soul rejoices in my God. For he has clothed me with garments of salvation and arrayed me in a robe of righteousness, as a bridegroom adorns his head like a priest, and as a bride adorns herself with her jewels. For as the soil makes the sprout come up and a garden causes seeds to grow, so the Sovereign Lord will make righteousness and praise spring up before all nations.

The Spirit of the Lord, God is upon Jesus. The Lord anointed Him to preach the Gospel of good news to the meek, the poor and afflicted. God's wisdom and revelation allowed

Jesus to bind up and heal men and women's hearts. He has given us access to receiving His promises. We receive victory by faith and love to see the fulfillment of the promise manifested in your situation. He is the comforter to those who grieve. He extends His favor of grace upon our lives. He gives leaps and boundless joy to those who grieve. He bestows His beauty upon you and your life He gives you for your ashes. He gives us lots of praise in place of sadness and sorrow. He is righteous making us righteous through a relationship with Him. He forgives us for our sins for the asking by faith in grace and not by works lest we boast. Ephesians 2:8,9. He is a just God. He makes us Oaks of righteousness planted in the Lord. May He be glorified.

He restores ancient ruins. He restores cities and blesses generations. People you do not know but I have placed them to feed your flocks and families. He calls us priests of the Lord. He is faithful and you shall eat the wealth of the nations. Also, the glory shall be yours because I do restore. God's blessing is twofold with recompense. First, you receive honor in place of dishonor. Second, you receive confidence in the Lord instead of your shame. Thirdly, you will rejoice in His faithful and loving portions giving you double for what you gave up. You shall receive everlasting joy. The Lord is a lover of justice. I disdain robbery and iniquity. I will be faithful and reward you. I made an everlasting covenant with you. Your offspring will be acknowledged and known among the nations. As well as your descendants in the midst of people. Those who see them in prosperity will realize and acknowledge that you have been blessed by the Lord, God Himself. God has clothed me with the clothes of salvation. He has placed a robe of righteousness as a beautiful bridegroom fancies himself with a garland and as a bride adorns herself with her jewels. Therefore, I am greatly rejoicing in Him and His pure beauty for my life.

God promises as surely as "the earth brings forth its shoots and as a garden causes what is sown in it to spring forth, so the Lord, God will cause rightness and justice and praise to spring forth before all the nations [through the self-fulfilling power of His word]."

➤ According to Isaiah 61:1 and Luke 4:18 the Spirit of the Lord is upon who?

___

➤ What did He anoint anoint Him to do according to Isaiah 61:1 & 2?

___

➤ What is the exchange according to Isaiah 61:3? Write out Isaiah 61:7.

___

➤ According to Isaiah 61:8 what does the Lord hate? And why? Why can you greatly rejoice according to Isaiah 61:10 & 11?

DAY 62

According to James 1:12 it states, "Blessed is the man who is patient under trial and stands up under temptation, for when he has stood the test and been approved, he will receive [the Victor's] Crown of Life, which God has promised to those who love Him.

To be patient in the testing of your faith is to persevere. When you go through it with God and finish it's work He makes you mature. He completes you and you lack nothing. James 1:4.

Henceforth, because you stood the test and have been approved by Him you will receive the Victor's Crown of Life. God promises this because you love Him even to the very end.

In your walk with the Lord there is a good fight. His endurance and love through you and your steadfast faith in Him and His promises gives you the will to complete the race. Thereby, there is in store for you a Crown of Righteousness. The Lord is the righteous Judge. He will reward you on that day because you loved Him. You also, looked forward to the day He would appear. II Timothy 4:8.

God is always fair. He is loving. He walks with you on a daily basis. He is with us throughout your life and for all eternity. He is righteous. As believer's His Spirit lives in you. He is Faithful. He loves. He will and knows your heart of obedience to Him. He will reward you with His Victorious Crown of Life. Henceforth, you will also wear a Crown of Righteousness by looking forward to the day He appears.

➤ According to James 1:12 what is promised to those who are patient and are approved and who stood the test of trial?

___

➤ According to James 1:4 why must perseverance finish its work?

___

➤ According to II Timothy 4:8 what happens when you keep the faith and finish His race for your life?

___

➤ How did the Lord speak to you in this lesson?

___

DAY 63

Psalm 63:1-8 states, *"O God you are my God, earnestly I seek you; my soul thirsts for you, my body longs for you, in a dry and weary land where there is no water. I have seen you in the sanctuary and beheld your power and your glory. Because your love is better than life, my lips will glorify you. I will praise you as long as I live, and in your name I will lift up my hands. My soul will be satisfied as with the richest of foods; with singing lips my mouth will praise you. On my bed I remember you; I think of you through the watches of the night. Because you are my help, I sing in the shadow of your wings. My soul clings to you; your right hand upholds me."*

David had a close relationship with the Lord. We too can have an intimate relationship that hungers, seeks, thirsts for God. Hunger is physical as well as what you desire. To seek is to find what is best for your soul (your mind, will and emotions). To thirst is to find you need God Himself. He is the only one that can satisfy your spirit and will meet your inner longings.

Like David we as believer's have seen and felt God's presence by lifting up the name of Jesus in praise and by lifting up God's word that feeds our souls. His presence of His love and goodness remains in His Holy Temple. God's rich endless love is better than life. Our response and heart proclaim as long as there is breathe in my body, my lips shall join with David and other believer's God shall be glorified. I will love and praise you in sweet surrender by lifting up my hands. I am being satisfied by God Himself with rich Manna. My lips sing to Him in joyful and grateful continual praise to God the Maker of Heaven and Earth.

God is remembered and I meditate upon your rich love and grace upon my bed and in the night time. You are my help and I sing from my heart endless praise.

Even in the shadow of your wings. My soul cleaves to you O God. Your right hand of strength uphold me. I will embrace you all the days of my life.

➤ How did David in Psalm 63:1 seek God?

➤ According to Psalm 63:3 why praise and glorify God?

➤ According to Psalm 63:5 what parts of the body will be satisfied with rich food and singing filled full of praise to God?

➤ How did God speak to you in Psalm 63:1-8?

DAY 64

Psalm 84 states, "How lovely is your dwelling place, O Lord Almighty! My soul yearns, even faints, for the courts of the Lord; my heart and my flesh cry out for the living God.

Even the sparrow has found a home, and the swallow a nest for herself, where she may have her young- a place near your altar, O Lord, Almighty my king and my God. Blessed are those who dwell in your house; they are ever praising you. Selah

Blessed are those whose strength is in you, who have set their hearts on pilgrimage. As they pass through the Valley of Baca, they make it a place of springs, the autumn rains also cover it with pools. They go from strength to strength till each appears before God in Zion.

Hear my prayer, O Lord Almighty; listen to me, O God of Jacob. Selah

Look upon our shield, O God; look with favor on your anointed one.

Better is one day in your courts then a thousand elsewhere; I would rather be a doorkeeper in the house of my God than dwell in the tents of the wicked.

For the Lord God is a sun and shield; the Lord bestows favor and honor, no good thing does He withhold from those whose walk is blameless. O Lord Almighty, blessed is the man who trusts in you."

Psalm 84 is a prayer to the Lord God Almighty (the Lord of Hosts). You are over all. My thoughts, will and emotions are full of love for your courts. My heart filled being cries and sings. You bring to me joy expressed to You the living God.

Even the birds are at home with you and are singing their love song to you. You are King, the Lord of Hosts. You are personal with me. I am joyful in your presence singing to you all day long. I love to praise You. You have become my strength. You and I fellowship together as you reveal to me your love, peace, joy, kindness, goodness, patience. I pursue You even in times of sadness. You comfort me and instill into me your character that perfects that which I am concerned about. You move me forward in springs of blessings. I gaze upon You and You instill into me Your countenance and character.

For a day in your courts is better than a thousand anywhere else. A doorkeeper in your house I would rather be than to live in the dwellings of evil. The Lord is light and sunshine protecting me from the rays of sun that are too hot. He keeps me on fire for Him. He continually gives me His grace and His heavenly splendor. For He is good to His children that run after Him and walk upright. I am blessed by Him trusting Him always.

➢ According to Psalm 84 what name is God?

_____
_____
_____
_____
_____

➢ According to Psalm 84:3 who feels at home with God?

_____
_____
_____
_____
_____

➢ According to Psalm 84:5-7 what is the result of passing through the Valley of Weeping?

_____
_____
_____
_____
_____

➢ How did the Lord speak to you in Psalm 84 a prayer to Him?

_____
_____
_____
_____
_____

DAY 65

Psalm 100 says, *"Shout for joy to the Lord, all the earth. Worship the Lord with gladness; come before Him with joyful songs. Know that the Lord is God. It is He who made us, and we are His; we are his people, the sheep of His pasture.*

Enter His gates with thanksgiving and His courts with praise; give thanks to Him and praise His name. For the Lord is good and His love endures forever; His faithfulness continues through all generations."

Joy filled praise songs come out of our heart to God Himself. We bow before Him. He is God. He designed and created us. We belong to Him. He is the Good Shepherd and I am in His pasture.

Come through His gates full of thankfulness. The place where He dwells full of praise to Him. The Lord is Good. His endless mercy and love are with us forever. He is faithful. His faithfulness goes on throughout all generations.

Psalm 93 says, *"The Lord reigns, He is robed in majesty; the Lord is robed in majesty and is armed with strength. The world is firmly established; it cannot be moved. Your throne was established long ago; You are from all eternity. The seas have lifted up, O Lord, the seas have lifted up their voice; the seas have lifted up their pounding waves. Mightier than the thunder of the great waters, mightier than the breakers of the sea- The Lord on high is mighty. Your statutes stand firm holiness adorns Your house for endless days, O Lord."*

The Lord does reign. The name of Jesus is above every name. Whatever situation you may be facing look to Him in glorious thankful praise. Worship Him as the King of your heart. The Lord is full of strength. He created the world firmly. His throne has been here and is established.

The Lord will always be here for He is everlasting. The seas voice is loud. The waves are pounding against the breakwater rocks. Yet, God is mightier. He is glorious. He is Holy. He alone is worthy of all praise. Let us bow down to Him: The Great I Am. Forever and ever. Amen!

➢ What is the theme of Psalm 100?

➢ According to Psalm 100 how do you enter His gates?

➢ According to Psalm 100 how do you enter His courts?

➢ According to Psalm 93 how does the Lord reign?

➢ How did the Lord speak to you through Psalm 100 & 93?

_____
_____
_____
_____
_____

The Lord spoke to me while going through a time of grieving the loss of two of God's servants of love who attended our church. George Hash and Nikki Tedesco who were instrumental in my life. In memory of them and what they are doing in heaven God gave me this song to share with other people who worship the Lord. It is named, "The Lord is King!"

THE LORD IS KING

4/4

D	F#	F#	F#
The	Lord	is	King

D major

D	F#	F#	F#
The	Lord	is	King

A	A	G	G	A	AG	G
He	Rules	and	Reigns		Forevermore	

D	F#	F#	F#
The	Lord	is	King

D	F#	F#	F#
The	Lord	is	King

A	A	G	G	A	AG	G
He	Rules	and	Reigns		Forevermore	

D	D	A	G	A	A	G	G
I	will	bow	down	and	Worship		Him

A	A	G	G A	A	G	A	A
He	is	so	worthy	is	so		worthy

D	F#	F#	F#	A	A G	G
The	Lord	is	clothed	with	majesty	

MERCIFUL: A DEVOTIONAL JOURNAL | 165

	A	A	G	G		A	G	A
	He's	robed	with	strength	and		power	

	D	F#	F#	F#		A	A	G G
	The	Lord	is	clothed		with		majesty

	A	A	G	G		A	G	A
	He's	robed	with	strength		and		power

	D	D	A	G	A	A	G	G
	I	will	bow	down	and	Worship		Him

	D	F#	F#	F#		A	G	A	A
	He	is	so	worthy		is	so		worthy

D	F#	F#	F4	A	A G	G	A A	G G
The	Lord	on	High	is	mightier	and		glorious

	A	G	A	G	A		AG
	Than	the	sounds	of		many	waters

D	F#	F#	F4	A	A G	G	A A	G G
The	Lord	on	High	is	mightier	and		glorious

	A	G	A	G	A		AG
	Than	the	sounds	of		many	waters

	D	D	A	G	A	A G		G
	I	will	bow	down	and	Worship		Him

	D	F#	F#	F#		A G	A	A
	He	is	so	worthy		is so		worthy

166 | SUSAN G. KABELITZ

D	F#	F#	F4	A	A		
I	will	give	him	my	heart		

G	G	A	A	G G	G	A G	G
My	soul	and	call	upon	His	Holy	name

D	F#	F#	F4	A	A		
I	will	give	him	my	heart		

G	G	A	A	G G	G	A G	G
My	soul	and	call	upon	His	Holy	name

D	D	A	G	A	A G	G	
I	will	bow	down	and	Worship	Him	

D	F#	F#	F#	A	G	A	A
He	is	so	worthy	is	so	worthy	

A	A	G	G	A G	A	A	
He	is	so	worthy	of all	my	praise	

A	A	G	G A	G	A	A	
He	is	so	worthy	of	all	praise	

THE LORD IS KING (PSALM 93)

THE LORD IS KING
THE LORD IS KING
HE RULES AND REIGNS FOREVERMORE

THE LORD IS KING
THE LORD IS KING
HE RULES AND REIGNS FOREVERMORE

I WILL BOW DOWN AND WORSHIP HIM
HE IS SO WORTHY IS SO WORTHY

THE LORD IS CLOTHED WITH MAJESTY
HE'S ROBED WITH STRENGTH AND POWER
THE LORD IS CLOTHED WITH MAJESTY
HE'S ROBED WITH STRENGTH AND POWER

I WILL BOW DOWN AND WORSHIP HIM
HE IS SO WORTHY IS SO WORTHY

THE LORD ON HIGH IS MIGHTIER AND GLORIOUS
THAN THE SOUNDS OF MANY WATERS
THE LORD ON HIGH IS MIGHTIER AND GLORIOUS
THAN THE SOUNDS OF MANY WATERS

I WILL BOW DOWN AND WORSHIP HIM
HE IS SO WORTHY IS SO WORTHY

I WILL GIVE HIM MY HEART
MY SOUL AND CALL UPON HIS HOLY NAME
I WILL GIVE HIM MY HEART
MY SOUL AND CALL UPON HIS HOLY NAME

I WILL BOW DOWN AND WORSHIP HIM
HE IS SO WORTHY OH SO WORTHY
HE IS SO WORTHY OF ALL MY PRAISE
HE IS SO WORTHY OF ALL PRAISE

INSPIRED BY THE HOLY SPIRIT 3-15-20
BY: SUSAN G. KABELITZ